STUDIES IN
COMPARATIVE ECONOMICS 6

Studies in Comparative Economics

INTERNATIONAL DIFFERENCES IN INDUSTRIAL STRUCTURE

EIGHT NATIONS IN THE 1950s

by Joe S. Bain

NEW HAVEN AND LONDON

YALE UNIVERSITY PRESS

1966

FOREWORD

Modern economics has been bred chiefly in Western Europe and the United States, and despite its aspiration toward generality it bears the stamp of institutions and issues characteristic of these areas.

But the economic world no longer revolves about London and New York. Dozens of new nations are struggling toward economic independence and industrial growth under institutional arrangements quite unlike those of the West. Economies of a novel type also extend eastward from central Europe to the Bering Strait and have been busily developing their own principles as a by-product of administrative experience. It is asserted that "Western economics" has only limited analytical value in these other countries.

The problem of the content and relevance of economics thus arises inescapably. Are the economic principles taught in the West really susceptible of general application? Or are they culture-bound and relevant mainly to industrial capitalist countries? Is it possible to create a general economics which would be as useful in Poland or India as in Canada or France? Or must we be content with several species of economics which will remain distinct in intellectual content and applicability?

"Comparative economics" has been regarded as a separate area of the economics curriculum, consisting of a botanical classification of national economies into a few loosely labeled boxes. But surely any course in economics is potentially comparative. A concern with comparative experience can profitably be infused into any of the standard branches of economic study. This series is inspired by the hope that a rethinking of particular branches of economics in world perspective, combined with a bibliography of available material from many countries, may help teachers to give their courses a broader and more comparative orientation.

In pursuing this objective, we deliberately chose autonomy over standardization. Each author was left free to determine his own approach and method of treatment. The essays thus differ considerably in length, analytical as against descriptive emphasis, geographical coverage, and other respects. How far the original intent of the series has been accomplished is for the profession to judge.

We are grateful to the authors who have struggled with possibly insoluble problems, to the Ford Foundation for its support of the enterprise, and to the staff of the Yale University Press for their helpful cooperation.

The Inter-University Committee on Comparative Economics: Abram Bergson, Arthur R. Burns, Kermit Gordon, Richard Musgrave, William Nicholls, Lloyd Reynolds (Chairman)

ACKNOWLEDGMENTS

The scope and purpose of this book are discussed in the first chapter. The basic research effort was greatly expedited by valuable advice from Professor Carlo Cipolla concerning Italy, from Professor Erik Lundberg concerning Sweden, and from Professor Henry Rosovsky concerning Japan. Systematic data on company concentration in Japanese industries were obtained from an English translation of an analysis of Japanese industrial statistics, done by the Japanese Fair Trade Commission, which was made available by Professor Corwin Edwards. The bulk of primary research and of organization and preliminary processing of data was done by Mrs. Belle Cole, an indefatigable and imaginative research economist whose assistance was invaluable in many ways, not the least of which was in discovering elusive foreign sources of essential data.

I should like to express my gratitude to the Inter-University Committee on Comparative Economics for its major support of the research effort, and to various of its members for helpful criticisms of the manuscript. Supplementary financial aid was generously provided by the Institute of Business and Economic Research at the University of California, Berkeley, and a year's appointment as a Ford Research Professor released the time needed for finally writing the book.

J. S. B.

Berkeley, California
November 2, 1965

CONTENTS

TABLES

Tables

APPENDIX TABLES

INTERNATIONAL DIFFERENCES
IN INDUSTRIAL STRUCTURE
EIGHT NATIONS IN THE 1950s

1 PREAMBLE

Rx: Please write a monograph on the comparative industrial organization of a sizable sample of countries or national economies, dealing with both their industrial structures and the economic performance of their industries. If possible, please extend your comparisons to apply to all non-agricultural industries, including not only manufacturing industries but also the distributive trades, the service trades, public utilities, and other urban industries. Also, please do not confine your sample to highly industrialized Western countries; girdle the globe and attempt to include countries in all the major geographical areas and in various stages of industrial development.

This prescription was offered to me in 1959 by the Inter-University Committee on Comparative Economics. I decided to try to fill it because it seemed like a good idea at the time and because the program of work suggested promised to be educational. To say that I did not fully anticipate the difficulties I was to encounter would clearly be an understatement.

It took only a few months to arrive at the firm conclusion, confirming a corresponding initial suspicion, that from all the books, monographs, governmental reports, and articles in existence dealing with the economies of various nations and their industrial sectors it would be impossible to assemble enough data to support a comparative analysis of the industrial organization of more than two or three countries which would be worth printing.

There is quite a lot of secondary literature of the sort mentioned, but in most of it the authors have given short shrift to the industrial organization of the country or countries with which they deal. So far as industrial organization is treated, comprehensive and systematic statistical descriptions are rare, and substantially undocumented horseback generalizations augmented with scattered tidbits of specific information are common. Also, in treating industrial organization the usual secondary sources confine their attention to general industrial structure and individual market structures (haphazardly covered), and almost never deal with economic performance in any specific fashion. Further, so far as industrial organization is considered, attention generally centers on the manufacturing sectors of national economies; there is very little indeed available on the distributive or the service trades, on utilities, on contracting, or on other nonfinancial sectors except agriculture.[1] At first, basing a judgment on my experience with the study of industrial organization in the United States, I may have been inclined to blame the manifold deficiencies of the existing literature on the laziness of the authors or on their lack of real interest

1. Some mention may be made also of the language barrier encountered in secondary source materials referring to some countries, such as Japan, which is a deterrent to a wide canvassing of potentially useful publications.

in industrial organization, but this was before I learned in detail about the sorts of primary data available to them.

Given the finding that available secondary sources were grossly inadequate as bases for the comparative study contemplated, three derivative conclusions followed. First, the comparisons involved would have to be developed in large part from primary data as found for various countries in censuses of industry or trade, in sources containing financial data for companies, and possibly from the managements of numerous leading firms, from trade associations, from members of foreign assistance missions, and so forth. Second, the primary contribution of the monograph would probably have to be the assembly and organization of systematic information on industrial structure and performance in a number of countries; any task of comparing and analyzing such information would be comparatively simple. Third, the primary objective should be to secure "hard" information, in the form of systematically developed statistics, so far as possible, and not to settle for broad characterizations, impressionistic generalizations, and the like. Thus began the interdependent search for a representative sample of countries and for adequate primary sources of data concerning individual countries.

One year, one research assistant, and hundreds of exchanges of correspondence later, several pertinent things had become painfully clear. Although I had begun with a tentative list of fifteen countries and a half-dozen alternates (other than the United States) as representative in all relevant ways of the national economies of the world—most of them considered "promising" because of good contacts with country specialists or native economists or, in two cases, because of the availability of good secondary works—the eligible members of the proposed sample fell away rapidly on account of the high frequency of cases in which no really useful and satisfactory data bearing on industrial organization were available at all, even within the limited sphere of industrial structure. Therefore the ultimate composition of the sample was determined in considerable part by the availability of data. Though several Western industrialized countries for which good data were available were passed by because of the prescription against loading the sample with such countries, we lost any representation on two major continents, Africa and South America (in spite of persistent efforts to salvage one Latin American country), and any representation of countries in the very early stages of industrial development. Similarly, we could not secure adequate data on any of the "iron curtain" countries (Russia having been set aside for special treatment in another monograph of this series). Therefore our final sample of eight countries, including the United States, though it covers a substantial range of country sizes, stages of industrial development, and degrees of settlement, is not representative in all essential respects and must be marked as including only countries with either free-enterprise economies or economies with quite limited socialization of industry, and only countries which have passed the earlier stages of industrialization. The sample of countries examined includes the United States, Canada, the United Kingdom, Sweden, France, Italy, India, and Japan.

A second thing that became clear was that for most countries even on such a "best data" list there was a substantial lack of usable data bearing on the economic performance of industries. Meaningful data on business profits, level and composition of costs, investments, and so forth are not in the public domain in most of the countries or, if in the hands of governmental agencies, have not been published or otherwise made available; and the private companies involved are not inclined to furnish such data to the inquiring scholar. Data on the productivity of labor and capital intensity in production such as are available are not generally in a form that accommodates meaningful analysis. It was thus reluctantly concluded after diligent and sustained efforts to unearth appreciable quantities of data bearing on the economic performance of industries in the seven countries other than the United States that no general comparisons of performance could be sustained. Therefore, the study was after initial stages of exploration focused almost entirely upon a comparison of the industrial structures of the eight countries studied. This monograph therefore is concerned narrowly with comparative industrial structure rather than more broadly with comparative industrial organization.

The only empirical findings concerning comparative market performance that we have been able to develop concern the comparative efficiency of industrial production so far as this is influenced by the scales of plants, and these are crude estimates based on the applications of certain norms of efficient plant scales developed from studies of American manufacturing industries. Otherwise our statistical analysis of industrial structures is augmented mainly by commentary on the probable relationship of variations among countries in company concentration and vertical integration to the incidence of monopolistic behavior, and on the probable significance for such behavior of nationalization and governmental control of industries where they are encountered.

With the focus on industrial structure, one further important limitation on available data was encountered. For practically all countries, reasonably adequate data on the structure of individual industries are available only for industries in the manufacturing sector. This is not surprising in view of the fact that the United States, with by far the best general industrial data of any country on earth, collects and publishes reasonably adequate data (other than for agriculture) only for manufacturing industries; our statistics on the distributive and service trades, on contracting, and on public utilities are distinctly inferior in coverage, detail, and general quality. The situation in the other countries studied ranges from no better through much worse to one of no data at all except for manufacturing. Although available data for each country do permit us to show the composition of the economy by sectors (manufacturing, trade, agriculture, etc.), they do not permit us to show the composition of sectors other than manufacturing by industries, and very definitely do not reveal the structures of individual industries outside of the manufacturing sector. In this study, therefore, we perforce deal with comparative industrial structure in the narrower sense, as the comparative composition by industries of the manufacturing sectors of the countries studied, and in particular as the comparative structures of individual manufacturing industries in the several countries.

The preceding brings us to the bedrock content of the findings about to be presented. Aside from some "backdrop" description of the sector breakdowns of national economies and of the industry breakdowns of national manufacturing sectors, we will be concerned with a description and comparison of the structures of individual manufacturing industries in the eight countries studied. As to dimensions of structure, we will confine ourselves almost entirely to size and to concentration, considered first for plants or establishments, and second for firms or other control units, in individual industries.

In our analysis of comparative plant structures of industries we will be concerned, for each of a substantial number of industries for all countries, with (1) the comparative sizes of plants, in general and for the larger plants in any industry; (2) the comparative degrees of plant concentration in every industry, considered as measures of the comparative technical bases of observed degrees of concentration of control of industries by firms; and (3) the comparative efficiency of industries so far as efficiency is affected by scale of plant. This analysis of plant structures is almost entirely an exercise in the presentation and interpretation of descriptive statistics; it requires only an insig-

Preamble

nificant fraction of the effort expended in assembling and
processing the primary data employed. The major departure
from routine statistical description occurs when we introduce
certain exterior norms of minimal efficient plant size in
order to make rough estimates of the proportions of workers
that are employed, in each country in each industry studied,
in plants of reasonably efficient scale.

In our analysis of the structure of industries by firms we
will be concerned, for each of a number of industries for
all countries, with the comparative degree of concentration
of control by firms or other control units—with the comparative incidence of substantial monopolies, concentrated
oligopolies, dilute oligopolies, and atomistic industries
among countries. These findings of course have primary relevance to issues of monopoly power. The bare statistical findings will require some special interpretation country by
country. In particular, we wish to examine the extent to
which existing degrees of concentration of control by firms
are justified or explained by existing plant concentration,
as this may be revealed by comparing company-concentration
and plant-concentration ratios. Further, we will consider the
probable significance of governmentally owned enterprises
within some industries in several countries, attempt to assess
the roles as control units of managing agencies in India and
zaibatsu in Japan, give notice to the apparent incidence of
cartelization, and, so far as data permit, interpret domestic
concentration by firms in various industries in various countries in the light of volumes of competitive imports. Considerably more attention to detail in individual countries
will thus be required in the analysis of the structure of industries by firms than in the counterpart analysis of plants.

In the analysis of firms we are fortunately able in general
to base our measures of concentration on output or sales
data. In the analysis of plants we are unfortunately forced
to accept number of workers employed as the only available
common denominator measure of plant sizes and plant con-

9

centration. Number of workers is a somewhat unsatisfactory proxy variable for output or capacity of plants, especially because of intercountry variations in productive techniques or methods and in degrees of vertical integration in production, but it is the best proxy variable we have.

The analysis of industrial structure in this study is not extended to cover dimensions of structure other than size and concentration. The scraps of pertinent information available would not support a comparable analysis of product differentiation in or of conditions of entry to industries, and time and resources available did not permit us to undertake the huge volume of research that would be required to develop appraisals of these dimensions of market structures.

The limited scope of our present inquiry having been generally described, let us now turn to the findings.

2 THE GENERAL COMPOSITION OF EIGHT NATIONAL ECONOMIES AND OF THEIR MANUFACTURING SECTORS

This study is concerned primarily with analyzing the structures of individual manufacturing industries in eight countries: the United States, Canada, the United Kingdom, Sweden, France, Italy, India, and Japan. Because we will be emphasizing only one aspect of the general economic structure of the countries under study, it seems appropriate to set this analysis in the context of a brief overview of a few general characteristics of the several national economies. Since this is not supposed to be a long book, we will not pause to describe the physical or economic geography, sociology, governmental system, or institutional peculiarities of any of these countries; they should be reasonably well known to the average reader, and atlases and encyclopedias are available. But we will give brief attention to the comparative populations of the countries, to the proportions of

11

their work forces employed in various sectors of economic activity, and to the compositions of their manufacturing sectors by industries.

The populations of the eight countries, circa 1960, are shown in Table 2–1. A wide range of country sizes as

TABLE 2–1

Populations of Countries Studied, circa 1960

Country	Population (in thousands)	Date of Census
United States	179,323	1960
Canada	18,238	1961
United Kingdom	52,676	1961
Sweden	7,495	1960
France	46,530	1962
Italy	50,464	1961
India	434,885	1961
Japan	93,419	1960

Source: United Nations Statistical Office, Department of Economic and Social Affairs, Statistical Yearbook, 1962 (New York, 1962). Population figures for the United States exclude armed services and civilian citizens absent from the country for an extended period of time; for the United Kingdom exclude Channel Islands and the Isle of Man; for Sweden include all citizens whether at home or abroad; for France, refer only to metropolitan France; for India include the Andaman, Nicobar, Laccadive, Minicoy, and Amindivi Islands, and exclude Kashmir and Jammu; for Japan, pertain to Hokkaido, Honshu, Shikoku, Kyushu, and the Amami Islands to the Kara Archipelago, and exclude personnel outside the country and allied military personnel and their dependents.

measured by population is evidently covered in our sample, ranging from about 7.5 million in Sweden to about 180 million in the United States and 435 million in India. France, Italy, and the United Kingdom are of the same general size, each with a population in the neighborhood of 50 million; Japan is almost twice this large and roughly half as large as the United States in population; Canada is relatively small. The proportions of population to land area vary widely among the countries.

The general structures of the several national economies are revealed in Table 2-2, which shows the distribution of the gainfully employed population, as measured in absolute numbers, among the major sectors of the economy for each country, and in Table 2-3, which shows for each country the percentage of the work force employed in each sector. The data in these tables refer to various years for various countries, ranging from 1950 to 1955; available data for substantially later years are incomplete. A general caveat must be entered to the effect that various intercountry differences in principles of enumeration (suggested by notes e through n to Table 2-2) are such that the tables will not support precise comparisons, though rough ones are in order. The following general similarities and differences in general economic organization among the eight countries seem to stand out.

First, if the proportion of the labor force employed in manufacturing were taken as an index of the degree of industrialization of a country, it would appear that the United Kingdom was the most highly industrialized of the countries under consideration; that Sweden ranked second with an appreciably lesser degree of industrialization; that the United States, Canada, and France, though highly industrialized, had about the same degrees of industrialization, in a range slightly below Sweden; that Italy and Japan had moderately lesser degrees of industrialization; and that India had the lowest, and an absolutely low, degree of industrialization. Second, however, if industrialization is more or less inversely proportional to the percentage of national work force employed in agriculture, the preceding judgments are not entirely borne out. The ranking of the United Kingdom as the most highly industrialized country is confirmed by the finding that of all the countries, it has the smallest percentage of its work force engaged in agriculture, and the ranking of India as least industrialized is consistent with the finding that over 70 per cent of its work force is agricultural. Al-

TABLE 2-2

Volume of Employment in the Major Sectors of the National Economy
for Each Country Studied, as of the Early 1950s

NUMBER OF PERSONS EMPLOYED (IN THOUSANDS)

Economic Sector[a]	United States[e]	Canada[f]	United Kingdom[g]	Sweden[h]	France[i]	Italy[j]	India[k]	Japan[l]
Manufacturing	14,685	1,361	9,416	978	4,937	4,521	12,554	6,969
Agriculture	7,033	1,007	1,154	632	5,213	8,261	100,627	16,099
Services[b]	12,606	1,006	5,026	529	3,228	2,693	14,628	5,701
Commerce[c]	12,427	854	1,742	403	2,640	1,535	7,310	6,019
Construction	3,458	351	1,523	245	1,357	1,472	1,468	1,813
Transport and communications	3,666	403	3,366	251	1,005	806	2,136	2,027
Other public utilities	785	62	384	29	135	109	—[m]	—[n]
Mining and quarrying	931	104	866	15	412	176	798	533
Not classifiable[d]	843	81	—	23	240	1,094	—	2
Total	56,434	5,229	23,477	3,105	19,167	20,667	139,521	39,163

[a] The sector classification conforms to the International Standard Industrial Classification of All Economic Activities, for which see International Labor Office, *Yearbook of Labor Statistics, 1962* (Geneva, 1962).

[b] Includes governmental, community, business, recreational, and personal services.

[c] Includes wholesale and retail trade, banks and other financial institutions, insurance, and real estate.

[d] Generally includes "persons seeking work for the first time" but does not include "unemployed workers."

[e] United States Bureau of the Census, *Census of Population, 1950, Summary Statistics* (Washington, 1951). Includes all civilians 14 years of age or older who were at work or with a job but not at work during the week the survey was taken. Reference date: 1950.

[f] International Labor Office, *Yearbook of Labor Statistics, 1951* (Geneva, 1952). Excludes the Yukon and Northwest Territories, the armed forces, and Indians living on reservations. "Not classifiable" includes activities not adequately described and persons seeking work for the first time. Reference date: 1951.

[g] Great Britain Central Statistical Office, *Annual Abstract of Statistics, 1955* (London, 1956). Includes all persons 15 years of age or older who work for pay or register themselves as available for work. Reference date: 1955.

[h] Quarrying is included in manufacturing rather than in mining in Swedish data. Reference date: 1950. Sweden, Board of Trade, *Industri, 1957* (Stockholm, 1957).

[i] The French data are based on a five per cent sample of census returns. Reference date: 1954.

[j] Italian data refer to persons 10 years of age or older and are based on a labor-force survey. Reference date: 1951.

[k] India Census Commissioner, *Census of India, 1951*, Vol. I-A (New Delhi, 1952). Includes self-supporting persons and earning dependents. Reference date: 1951.

[l] Japanese data refer to persons 15 years of age or older and are based on a one per cent sample of census returns. "Not classifiable" includes activities not adequately described. Reference date: 1955.

[m] "Other public utilities" are included with "Services."

[n] "Other public utilities" are included with "Transport and communications."

General source: United Nations Statistical Office, Department of Economic and Social Affairs, *Statistical Yearbook, 1957* (New York, 1957), except where otherwise noted in notes above.

TABLE 2–3

Percentages of the Work Force in the Major Sectors of the National Economy
for Each Country Studied, as of the Early 1950s[a]

PERCENTAGE OF THE NATIONAL WORK FORCE

Economic Sector	United States	Canada	United Kingdom	Sweden	France	Italy	India	Japan
Manufacturing	26.1	26.0	40.1	31.5	25.8	21.9	9.0	17.8
Agriculture	12.5	19.2	4.9	20.4	27.2	40.0	72.1	41.1
Services	22.3	19.1	21.5	17.0	16.8	13.0	10.5	14.5
Commerce	22.0	16.2	7.4	13.0	13.8	7.4	5.2	15.4
Construction	6.1	6.6	6.5	7.9	7.1	7.1	1.1	4.6
Transport and communications	6.5	7.6	14.3	8.1	5.2	3.9	1.5	5.2
Other public utilities	1.4	1.8	1.6	0.9	0.7	0.5	—[b]	—[c]
Mining and quarrying	1.6	2.0	3.7	0.5	2.1	0.9	0.6	1.4
Not classifiable	1.5	1.5	—	0.7	1.3	5.3	—	negl.[d]
Total	100.0	100.0	100.0	100.0	100.0	100.0	100.0	100.0

[a]All notes to Table 2–2 are applicable here.   [c]Included with "Transport and communica-
[b]Included with "Services."   tions."
                                                   [d]Negligible.

Sources: Same as those of Table 2–2.

though Canada, Sweden, and France all have proportions of their labor forces engaged in manufacturing comparable to this proportion in the United States, they all have from moderately to very substantially higher proportions of their work forces engaged in agriculture than does the United States. And Italy and Japan, though lagging behind the United States only moderately in industrialization as measured by proportion of work force employed in manufacturing, devote proportions of their work forces to agriculture which are over three times the corresponding proportion in the United States. Five of the seven countries that appear from their manufacturing employment data to be from moderately to very highly industrialized are thus also from highly to moderately agrarian in their total economic activity.

The disparities noted are of course accounted for mainly by the fact that in these countries which are ambivalently classified with regard to degree of industrialization the proportions of labor forces devoted to the distributive trades and other commerce and to the service trades are substantially smaller than the proportion devoted to these trades in the United States. This is true also even of the highly industrialized United Kingdom. No other country except Canada closely approaches the United States in terms of the proportion of manpower devoted to "commerce" and "services" combined. This fact probably reflects in general both the substantially higher per capita income of the United States and the much greater productivity of labor in its agriculture. It also reflects a higher degree of urbanization and in some sense a higher degree of overall industrialization than found in most of the other countries.

If we choose as an index of industrialization of a country the proportion of the work force employed in manufacturing, commerce, and the service trades combined, we obtain the following ranking of the eight countries:

United States	70.4
United Kingdom	69.0
Sweden	61.5
Canada	61.3
France	56.4
Japan	47.7
Italy	42.3
India	24.7

This index may not be entirely satisfactory as a means of comparing degrees of industrial-urban development, but it seems to place the eight countries in about their proper ranks in terms of "state of industrial development."[1] The reader is invited to make finer comparisons by referring to Tables 2–2 and 2–3.

In reviewing the general structures of the eight national economies, emphasis has been placed on degree of industrialization because of our primary concern in this study with the comparative structures of manufacturing industries and because intercountry differences in the degree of industrialization and urbanization could be associated with intercountry differences in the structures of various manufacturing industries. Before turning to the examination of manufacturing-industry structures, let us take one further preliminary step by comparing the compositions by major industry groups of the manufacturing sectors of the eight countries under consideration. This comparison is undertaken in Table 2–4, which shows for each country the percentages of manufacturing workers employed in each of twenty major industry categories, together with the total numbers of workers in manufacturing. The latter figures do not tally exactly with those in Table 2–2 for manufacturing sectors because different sources referring to slightly different dates

1. It should be noted that India and Japan maintain commerce and service trade sectors as large as they do (as measured in terms of employment) because these sectors absorb "labor surpluses" at low wages; their size has been referred to as "poverty induced" rather than "prosperity induced."

and using somewhat different principles of enumeration were used as bases for Table 2–4. Two columns are devoted to India because of the existence of two sources with greatly different degrees of coverage, the one with the greater coverage supporting less detailed showings.

The general picture developed in Table 2–4 is one of more or less fully diversified manufacturing in all of the countries except India, which has a low degree of development in the basic metal industries, in the fossil fuels industries, and in the transportation equipment and machinery categories, and has over half of its manufacturing activity concentrated in textiles and in food products. Canada is somewhat less diversified in manufacturing than other countries with a high general degree of industrial development. There is a general tendency for the proportionate importance of iron and steel and transportation equipment manufacturing to decline as we move from the more to the less highly industrialized countries, and for the proportionate importance of textile manufacturing to increase, the United Kingdom offering the principal exception to the latter tendency.

The United States appears to have attained a fairly well-balanced diversification in manufacturing activities. Taking it as a standard, we may note the following tendencies toward "specialization" or disproportionate emphasis in given lines of manufacturing in the other countries. The United Kingdom is heavily developed in transportation equipment, nonelectrical machinery, and textiles. Sweden has a disproportionate emphasis on manufacturing nonelectrical machinery and paper products. Canada has a similarly heavy development in nonferrous metals, lumber and wood, paper products, and food products. France has a disproportionate development in textile and fabricated metal product manufacturing. Japan, Italy, and especially India all have a heavy emphasis on textile manufacturing, and the manufacture of apparel is particularly large in Italy. A more detailed interpretation of Table 2–4 is left to the reader.

19

TABLE 2–4

Percentages of the Manufacturing Work Force in Twenty Major Manufacturing-Industry Categories for Each Country Studied, circa 1955

PERCENTAGE OF THE NATIONAL MANUFACTURING WORK FORCE

Manufacturing-Industry Category	United States[a]	United Kingdom[b]	Sweden[c]	Canada[d]	France[e]	Japan[f]	Italy[g]	India (1)[h]	India (2)[s]
Iron and steel	6.2	5.0	5.0	2.6	5.0	4.4	2.7	1.5	—
Nonferrous metals	0.9	1.3	0.8	4.0	0.8	1.5	0.8	0.2	—
Petroleum and oil	1.4	0.4	0.4	1.3	6.1	0.6	0.5	0.1	—
Nonmetallic minerals	3.1	3.9	4.7	3.0	3.7	5.1	5.9	4.0	7.6
Transportation equipment	11.0	16.9	9.7	10.6	10.3	6.2	5.4	4.2	—
Nonelectrical machinery	9.9	12.1	16.4	2.8	3.0	7.5	16.1	0.7	—
Electrical machinery	6.1	5.6	6.3	6.0	4.3	4.7	2.7	4.9	—
Fabricated metal products	6.5	5.7	8.3	9.2	11.3	4.8	0.7	3.8	—
Instruments	1.7	1.6	0.5	—	0.3	1.7	1.5	—	—
Chemicals and allied products	4.7	5.3	4.3	4.0	4.9	6.4	4.3	5.2	—
Rubber	1.6	1.3	1.4	1.7	1.3	1.3	1.1	1.0	4.0
Leather	2.3	0.8	2.4	2.3	1.4	0.8	1.1	1.0	10.5
Lumber and wood	4.1	1.6	6.5	9.4	2.3	6.9	5.5	0.9	
Furniture and fixtures	2.2	1.8	1.7	—	1.8	2.3	2.9	—	
Paper and allied products	3.4	2.2	7.1	6.9	2.1	3.1	1.8	0.8	0.4
Food and kindred products	10.6	9.5	7.8	14.1	7.0	12.6	10.2	13.8	21.5
Textiles	6.6	11.3	6.0	6.6	13.9	18.6	18.5	42.5	35.4
Apparel	7.6	7.4	5.7	6.7	6.7	3.0	11.8	0.1	
Tobacco	0.6	0.5	0.2	0.7	0.2	0.4	1.6	5.5	3.5
Printing and publishing	5.1	4.0	4.8	5.5	3.0	4.6	2.1	2.6	0.9
Miscellaneous	4.4	1.8	—	2.6	10.6	3.5	2.8	7.2	4.5
Chemicals, petroleum-coal, rubber									2.7
Iron and steel, fabricated metal products, nonferrous metals									7.2

Transportation equipment and electrical machinery

								1.8
Total	100.0	100.0	100.0	100.0	100.0	100.0	100.0	100.0	100.0
Total employment (in thousands)	15,651	9,102	835	1,359	4,872	6,196	3,502	3,145	16,202

[a] United States Bureau of the Census, *Census of Manufactures, 1954*, Vol. I, *Summary Statistics* (Washington, D.C., 1955). Includes for a specified pay period full- and part-time employees, employees on paid holidays and vacations in all categories, including production workers, supervisory staff, central office employees, employees in all nonproduction departments or offices. Excludes members of the armed forces, pensioners, proprietors and partners of unincorporated firms, working proprietors with no employees.

[b] United Kingdom, Central Statistical Office, *Annual Abstract of Statistics*, Vol. 99 (London, 1961). Reference date: year beginning May 1955. Coverage approximately the same as for United States, but working proprietors and partners of unincorporated firms are included.

[c] Sweden, Board of Trade, *Industri, 1957* (Stockholm, 1959). Coverage roughly the same as for United States, but includes working proprietors, excludes home workers, and excludes establishments employing five or fewer workers. Reference date: 1957.

[d] Canada, Dominion Bureau of Statistics, *General Review of Manufacturing Industries of Canada, 1957* (Ottawa, 1960). Reference date: 1956. Coverage roughly the same as for United States, but includes working proprietors of unincorporated establishments. See also Dominion Bureau of Statistics, *Iron & Steel Review*, 1957.

[e] France, Institut National de la Statistique et des Études Économiques, *Les Établissements industriels, artisaneaux et commerceaux en France en 1958* (Paris, 1959). Coverage roughly the same as for United States.

[f] Japan, Bureau of Statistics, *Statistical Yearbook, 1962* (Tokyo, 1963). Reference date: 1954. Coverage roughly the same as for United States, but includes proprietors and unpaid family workers.

[g] Italy, Instituto Centrali di Statistics, *Annuario statistico italiano, 1962* (Rome, 1963). Reference date: 1951. Coverage roughly the same as for United States.

[h] India, Planning Commission, Scientific and Technical Manpower and Perspective Planning Division, *Occupational Pattern in Manufacturing Industry, 1956* (New Delhi, 1959). The data cover registered establishments using power and employing 10 or more workers, or not using power and employing 20 or more workers. Based on a sample survey covering about 17 per cent of such establishments and 58 per cent of such workers.

[i] Ibid., and P. N. Dhar and H. F. Lydal, *The Role of Small Enterprise in Indian Manufacturing* (Bombay, 1961). These data are based on estimates from a special tabulation prepared by the Perspective Planning Division of the Planning Commission of India, and were taken from the Ninth Round of the National Sample Survey Commission (May–November, 1955). They include establishments with power employing less than 10 workers and those without power employing less than 20 workers. They include earning dependents, unpaid family workers, and manufacturing employment in general in household enterprises and small workshops, these accounting for about two-thirds of total Indian manufacturing employment. Various industry categories for which no employment is shown in the second column for India are included in aggregates shown in the last three rows of the table.

In interpreting Table 2–4, it must be remembered that it shows employment only by broad industry categories, and that most of these categories contain at least several separate "industries" as the term industry is ordinarily used in economic analysis, or several "four-digit" industries according to the classification used in the Census of Manufactures of the United States. Thus, for example, the nonferrous metals industry category includes the aluminum, copper, lead, zinc, and other industries, and the chemicals and allied products category includes several distinct basic industrial chemical industries, synthetic fibers, plastics, paints and varnishes, and so forth.

The degree of diversification by individual industries more properly and more narrowly defined is evidently not as great in most of the countries under study as Table 2–4 might suggest. Deficiencies in the censuses of manufacture in most of the countries, however, make it difficult to determine for them how many "four-digit" industries exist in each broad industry category.

It should be noted in conclusion that the data on Indian manufacturing are especially unsatisfactory, largely because of the considerable importance in that country of cottage industry and the difficulties encountered in making censuses of such industry. (Comparable though much lesser difficulties are encountered in Japan, but there a relatively firm census including household industry has been made.) Two columns of data are thus presented showing the composition of Indian manufacturing. The first column, India (1), in Table 2–4 excludes cottage industry, and also all establishments using power and employing less than 10 workers. It thus accounts for only a part of the manufacturing economy of India and apparently for less than a fifth of the Indian population engaged in manufacturing. The second column, India (2), includes all cottage industry and perhaps overgenerously, and reflects estimates based on a sample survey. It gives us a manufacturing work force of about 16 million as opposed to about 3 million for the more restricted census, and is notable in that it indicates for all Indian manufacturing a substantially heavier emphasis than does the first India column on leather and leather products, lumber and wood products, food and allied products, nonmetallic mineral products, and fabricated metal products, and a proportionally reduced emphasis in most of the other industrial categories. The areas of increased emphasis in the second column are clearly the provinces of household and small workshop industry in India, and together account for a high proportion of its manufacturing employment. Indian manufacturing as a whole appears substantially more diversified when cottage industry is taken into account. The data in the second column on Indian manufacturing in Table 2–4, however, should be regarded as supplying no more than rough indications of the volume and composition of Indian manufacturing employment, and as potentially subject to significant errors. Substantially all censuses of manufactures of all countries of course are shot through with minor errors of enumeration and of classification.

The preceding comparison of countries in terms of the general compositions of their manufacturing sectors provides a backdrop for the intercountry comparison of major aspects of the plant structures of individual industries, which we will now consider.

3 COMPARATIVE PLANT SIZE AND CONCENTRATION IN SELECTED MANUFACTURING INDUSTRIES

The plant structure of any manufacturing industry may be measured in several dimensions, principal among which are plant sizes in absolute terms, plant concentration, and the degree of intraplant vertical integration. We have been able to obtain systematic information for countries outside the United States only on plant size and plant concentration, and are thus able to offer nothing concerning intraplant vertical integration.

Plant concentration within an individual industry is generally described by the absolute number and the proportionally measured size distribution of plants within the industry. It is most readily measured for summary purposes in any industry by the percentages of the total capacity, output, or employment of the industry accounted for by various absolute numbers of "largest" plants in the industry. If all plants in an industry are arrayed in order of decreasing size (size being measured by capacity, output, or employment), and the size of each plant noted, the plant concentration pattern may be summarized for example by calculations of the percentages of total industry capacity, output, or employment accounted for by the largest four plants (the top four in the array), the largest eight plants, the largest twenty, largest fifty, and so forth. The degree of plant concentration in any industry is primarily relevant to economic analysis in that it reveals the existing technical basis of the going degree of concentration of control of an industry by firms or other control units. If a firm can control no less than one plant, firm concentration cannot be less than plant concentration unless existing plants can be dismembered or reduced in size, but it may be substantially greater. The degree of plant concentration in an industry suggests a feasible minimum for firm concentration, or that minimal degree of firm concentration which is "required" by existing plant concentration. And the extent of divergence between plant concentration and firm concentration in an industry may be taken as indicative of the extent to which existing firm concentration is not "justified" or explained by existing plant concentration. The comparative degrees of plant concentration for different industries in the same country, or for the same industry or group of industries in different countries, correspondingly reveal the comparative technical bases for comparative degrees of concentration of industry control by firms.[1]

The absolute sizes of plants in an industry, as measured in terms of capacities, outputs, or numbers of workers employed, comprise another dimension of the plant structure

1. These technical bases for company concentration are not necessarily the same thing as technological justifications for such concentration. Some of the largest plants in an industry may be larger than required for optimal efficiency (though usually not less efficient thereby), and from a minor to a major fraction of industry output may be supplied by plants of inefficiently small scale.

of an industry. This dimension of plant structure can be fully revealed only by listing the absolute sizes of all plants in the industry, as arrayed in order of size. It can be summarized for any industry by calculating for example the average size of the largest four plants, of the largest eight, twenty, and fifty plants, and of all plants (as well as of the average sizes of various intermediate numbers of "largest" plants). The absolute sizes of the plants in any industry have little economic significance unless interpreted in the light of other information such as that concerning the minimum optimal size of a plant in that particular industry and the degrees of inefficiency associated with plants of smaller size. Given such information, the distribution of plant sizes in an industry can be analyzed to determine what proportion of industry output is being supplied by plants of reasonably efficient scale. A comparison of the absolute sizes of plants in different industries is relatively meaningless. However a comparison of the absolute sizes of plants in the same industry in different countries may provide the basis, given some supplementary information, for inferences concerning the comparative efficiency of an industry in different countries, so far as efficiency is affected by size of plants.

The basic statistical data from which measures of plant concentration and plant size for individual industries have been developed consist of frequency distributions for individual industries which show, for each national industry listed: (1) the number of plants in each of a series of size classes, where size is measured by number of employees in a plant; and (2) the number of employees in each size class of plants. (Number of employees is the only size measure for plants employed in common in the statistics of most countries.) Uniformly for all countries a manufacturing plant or "establishment" is defined as a unified complex of production facilities on a single site—a single factory, mill, refinery, works, shop, etc. A typical size distribution is of the following general character (the one shown refers to the plastics

26

materials industry of the United States in 1958, from the 1958 Census of Manufactures):

Number of Employees in a Plant	Number of Plants	Number of Employees
1–19	153	1,094
20–49	74	2,359
50–99	41	2,830
100–249	38	6,857
250–499	18	6,057
500–999	11	7,688
1,000–2,499	11	15,863
2,500 and over	3	8,255
Total	349	51,003

The available plant data, drawn from separate national censuses of manufactures or industry for each of the separate countries, generally appear in no more refined a form than the preceding.

This being the case, it is evident that uniform indices of plant concentration applying to all industries and countries (such as the percentages of workers employed by the largest four, eight, twenty, and fifty plants) and uniform measures of absolute plant sizes (such as the average number of employees of the largest four, eight, twenty, and fifty plants) cannot be read directly from the available data. Instead, such concentration indices and plant-size measures must be estimated by some procedure for each country. The procedure employed here has been to obtain for any desired measure the *statistically possible* maximum value and the *statistically possible* minimum value, and to accept the arithmetic mean of these maximum and minimum values as an estimate of the value sought.

One example may suffice to illustrate the general procedure of estimation employed. Suppose that from the frequency distribution above we wish to estimate the percentage of workers employed in the largest twenty plants in the industry. From the distribution we observe that the fourteen largest plants unequivocally employ 24,118 workers out of the industry total of 51,003. Our problem is to estimate the number of workers controlled by the six largest plants smaller than the first fourteen—i.e. the six largest in the class interval of plants employing 500–999 workers. The smallest number of workers that it is statistically possible for these six plants to employ is that which would occur if all eleven plants in the 500–999 plant-size class were of equal size. If this were so, the average size of the six "largest" plants would be the number of workers in the class divided by the number of plants in it, or $(7,688 \div 11) = 699$. The six largest plants would then control six times 699 workers, or 4,194 workers; this is the smallest number of workers they could possibly employ. The largest number of workers that it is statistically possible for the six plants to control is either the number of workers they would employ if each were at the upper limit of the size class (999 workers per plant) or the number of workers they would control if all the remaining smaller plants in size class were at the lower limit of the size class, whichever is smaller. Thus we have two estimates of the maximum possible employment of the six plants in question: (a) 999 multiplied by 6, or 5,994; and (b) the total number of workers in the class, 7,688, minus 500 multiplied by 5 (which is 2,500), or 5,188. The lower maximum estimate of 5,188 workers controlled by the six largest firms in the class is accepted since the higher estimate of 5,994 is statistically impossible; if the six largest plants each employed 999 workers, or 5,994, there could be only 1,694 workers employed by the smaller five plants, or 339 each, which would place them below the lower limit of the size class in which they are placed, or below 500 workers each.

We now have two estimates of the number of workers controlled by the largest twenty plants in the industry: 24,118 plus 4,194, and 24,118 plus 5,188, or 28,312 and 29,306. The corresponding minimum and maximum statistically possible percentages of all industry workers employed by the largest twenty plants are 55.5 and 57.5 per cent, and the mean estimate is halfway between these two, at 56.5 per cent.

The general procedure of estimation illustrated above has been employed throughout in calculating plant concentration indices, average sizes for given absolute numbers of plants, and related measures, with appropriate adaptations in treating open-end categories in size distributions and in estimating the number of plants required to account for 50 per cent of industry employment. The maximum and minimum estimates of a value are not always so close together as in the preceding example, so that there is frequently room for significant error in an estimate calculated as the mean of such statistically possible maximum and minimum values. The estimation procedure employed implicitly assumes a given shape of the size distribution of plant sizes, and this assumption may not be fulfilled. Empirically, the procedure appears to be as accurate as any comparably simple one. In a recent study, plant concentration indices for a large sample of United States manufacturing industries have been computed from detailed census data for 1954, representing precise measures rather than estimates.[2] They permit direct comparisons with our estimates of United States plant concentration in the same year for about 18 of 34 industries included in our comparative analysis, based on frequency distributions of the same data. In about half of the cases our estimates of four-plant concentration are quite close to the actual concentration indices or within 10 per cent of the true figures. In about a quarter of cases they are significantly higher and in about a quarter significantly lower, diverging from the true figures by more than 10 per cent and frequently by 25 per cent or more.[3] The error in

2. Ralph L. Nelson, *Concentration in Manufacturing Industries in the United States* (New Haven, 1963), Appendix Table A–4.

3. By a 10 per cent divergence we refer to a percentage difference between the true percentage controlled by x plants and the estimated

our estimates moreover declines (as would be expected) as we proceed through concentration indices referring to progressively larger absolute numbers of plants. It is mainly for this reason that in the following presentation we will center our attention on estimates of concentration indices and absolute plant sizes referring to the largest twenty plants in various industries, though comparable estimates have been completed referring to the largest four and eight plants.

Because of unavoidable errors inherent in our estimating procedures, the findings should be viewed as rough-and-ready indications of tendencies rather than as precise measures. The precise data available for the United States were not used because comparable data were not available for other countries (and incomplete for the United States) and because in this circumstance it seemed desirable to apply identical estimating procedures to the data for all countries.

The estimates of comparative plant concentration and comparative absolute plant size presented below refer to a sample of 34 manufacturing "industries" for which data for all or most of the eight countries compared could be secured, and for which the definition or scope of the industry, in terms of product or products manufactured, was approximately the same for all countries. The high incidence of nonmatching industry classifications as among different countries severely restricted the scope of the sample, but within the limits thus imposed we have endeavored to secure a representation of most of the major manufacturing categories by one or more narrowly defined industries, such as "four-digit" industries according to the classification of the Census of Manufactures of the United States. Though our initial intention was to begin with a full roster of United

---

percentage controlled by the same number of plants. Thus if the true concentration ratio (percentage) is 30 and the estimated concentration ratio is 33, the divergence in our terms is 10 per cent (of 30), but only 3 *percentage points*.

States four-digit industries and select those industries for which comparable data were available for most or all of the other countries, we have been forced, in view of the industry classification systems pursued by other countries, to include in our sample three two-digit industry categories and a few categories which combine two or more four-digit industries according to the United States classification.

All of the basic data on which we have drawn in estimating plant sizes and indices of plant concentration are summarized and annotated in Appendix Tables A–1 through A–8. We present here in Table 3–1 a list of the industries in the sample for which plant structures have been analyzed and, as available, the number of employees in each industry in each of the eight countries studied. From this table the reader should gain a general idea of the industry coverage of the sample and of the absolute and relative importance of the various industries in different countries.

For general industry definitions, and a description of intercountry variances in definition, the reader is referred to the notes to the Appendix tables. No general interpretation of Table 3–1 seems necessary. It may be noted in passing however: (1) that in most of the industries the United States has the largest national employment, with the United Kingdom generally running second and Japan most frequently third; (2) that there are significant exceptions to this rule involving nonferrous metals, shipbuilding, hardware, explosives, pulp, seafood, and wool textiles, in many of which industries the United Kingdom or Japan or both have larger national employment (though Canada takes first rank in wood pulp and four countries have larger woolen textile industries); (3) that in four industries in India in which cottage industry is predominant (tobacco products, saw and planing mills, grain products, and sugar refining), that country has by far the largest national manufacturing employment of any of the eight countries when cottage industry is counted (as it is in Table 3–1), and that this may

31

TABLE 3–1

List of Thirty-four Industries for Which Plant Size and Concentration are Compared, with Total Employment by Countries

Industries	United States	United Kingdom	Sweden	Canada	France	Japan	Italy	India[a]
				NUMBER OF EMPLOYEES (IN THOUSANDS)				
Steel works and rolling mills	482.2	211.9	34.0	33.6	187.3	56.6	25.1	93.9
Nonferrous metals	54.5	112.1	4.9	36.0	16.6	111.3	25.9	7.0
Petroleum refining	153.1	16.4	1.8	11.6	20.5	10.4	8.8	3.0
Cement	39.8	12.8	1.7	n.a.	24.3	18.7	24.9	24.2
Glass products	137.5	65.4	6.1	n.a.	47.5	49.8	36.0	24.3
Motor vehicles and parts	695.5	379.4	n.a.	32.5	183.5	143.0	76.6	69.8
Aircraft	822.5	241.7	n.a.	41.6	62.8	9.8	6.4	6.1
Shipbuilding	125.3	220.5	27.2	n.a.	87.0	145.7	39.8	28.4
Agricultural machinery	139.1	n.a.[b]	n.a.	n.a.	33.3	30.1	14.7	n.a.
Electrical industrial equipment	775.3	311.4	35.2	81.2	168.5	135.1	n.a.	n.a.
Electric light bulbs	22.0	15.5	n.a.	n.a.	9.4	11.5	6.7	n.a.
Hardware	128.6	212.6	n.a.	n.a.	91.3	53.9	20.6	n.a.
Explosives	32.5	40.7	3.1	n.a.	26.6	7.5	7.5	n.a.
Plastics	41.1	22.0	3.6	n.a.	n.a.	n.a.	4.1	7.1
Paints and varnishes	70.0	37.9	1.7	n.a.	15.2	9.2	8.3	5.8
Drugs	92.0	49.2	1.1	n.a.	34.8	48.3	28.5	n.a.
Soap	46.3	22.1	2.1	n.a.	8.1	12.0	17.6	9.5

Industry	United States	United Kingdom	France	Japan	India	Canada	Sweden	Italy
Tobacco products	94.9	41.3	1.3	9.9	10.0	n.a.	51.2	570.7
Sawmills and planing mills	321.2	102.4	26.2	50.0	112.8	273.4	32.2	1,646.9
Wood containers	52.3	26.7	1.0	n.a.	n.a.	44.9	19.9	n.a.
Pulp mills	57.7	n.a.	20.2	63.2	17.3	15.1	n.a.	n.a.
Paper and paperboard	142.2	78.2	21.5	n.a.	29.0	83.6	40.8	27.7
Grain products	109.9	35.5	1.4	11.1	38.3	34.3	63.4	410.7
Sugar refining	30.2	18.7	2.2	n.a.	39.1	9.2	11.8	517.2
Canned and preserved fruits, vegetables	148.3	54.0	5.0	17.4	21.8	24.7	19.7	2.8
Seafood (canned, packaged, cured)	29.1	6.7	2.5	13.2	14.6	124.4	4.3	n.a.
Breweries	83.9	68.3	5.1	n.a.	17.7	6.1	4.5	5.7
Distilled liquor	21.5	5.1	1.3	n.a.	13.3	19.4	15.5	n.a.
Cotton textiles	269.2	104.7	n.a.	n.a.	n.a.	195.1	136.5	n.a.
Wool textiles	87.3	196.4	9.3	n.a.	141.0	132.4	124.6	16.4
Knitting mills	221.3	122.8	8.9	n.a.	90.1	82.0	84.4	10.5
Leather tanning	43.5	31.6	2.2	n.a.	27.8	10.3	18.4	20.2
Rubber products	246.5	106.3	7.8	22.2	60.8	89.6	38.5	30.9
Apparel	972.7	422.5	38.9	90.6	317.8	155.1	411.1	2.4

[a]Data for India refer to manufacturing in establishments with 10 or more workers with power and 20 or more workers without power except for the following categories for which cottage industry and very small plants are very important: sawmills and planing mills, tobacco products, paper and paperboard, grain products, sugar refining. For these industries, data cover all manufacturing establishments. (See Appendix Table A–8.)

[b]Not available.

Sources and definitions of industry categories: See Appendix Tables A–1 to A–8.

Years of reference: United States, United Kingdom, France, 1954; Japan, India, 1956; Canada, Sweden, 1957; Italy, 1951.

be true of a few other industries for which a separate count of Indian cottage-industry employment is not available; and (4) that the pattern of relatively balanced diversification of industrial development by individual countries which is suggested by Table 2–4, showing national employment by broad industry categories, is not sustained as we examine data referring to more narrowly defined manufacturing industries as shown in Table 3–1. The detailed composition of manufacturing activity varies quite significantly among the eight countries in general. Some of the concomitants of wide differences in individual industry size among countries, in the form of differences in absolute plant sizes and in degrees of plant concentration, appear below.

COMPARATIVE PLANT SIZES

As a backdrop for consideration of comparative plant concentration in the industries sampled among the eight countries, and for future reference in other connections, it should be useful to present first some data on the comparative absolute sizes of plants in various industries among the countries under examination. This comparison of absolute sizes of plants could be presented in considerable detail—for example by showing for each industry for each country the estimated average number of employees in the largest four, eight, twenty, and fifty plants, and in all plants. We have indeed calculated a full set of such estimates, but as presented they would constitute a complex jumble of numbers which would be difficult to read and more difficult to interpret. After examining our detailed estimates we have concluded that the general order of intercountry differences with respect to individual plant sizes in various industries is roughly indicated in a satisfactory fashion (except so far as cottage industry is importantly involved) by comparing the countries for each industry with respect to the estimated average number of employees in the twenty largest plants in the national industry (the estimated total employment in the twenty largest plants divided by twenty). The data that we present in Table 3–2 are derived from estimates of the following general type, as illustrated for canning and preserving of fruits and vegetables:

Country	Estimated Average Number of Employees in the Twenty Largest Plants	Estimated Comparative Size of the Twenty Largest Plants
United States	1,320	100
United Kingdom	1,010	77
Sweden	111	8
Canada	327	25
France	255	19
Japan	219	17
Italy	201	15
India	112	8

Such estimates for each industry represent the arithmetic means of statistically possible maximum and statistically possible minimum average sizes of the largest twenty plants in the eight countries, as calculated from available frequency distributions of plant sizes by the general method described above, on pages 26 to 30. For presentation in the interest of easy interpretation, all such estimates for each industry have been converted into relatives based on the average plant size for the United States as 100, as shown in the third column of the tabulation above. In Table 3–2, therefore, we show not the estimated *absolute* sizes of the largest twenty plants for each industry for each country, but for each industry the *comparative* average sizes of the largest twenty plants for each country. In those instances where a country has fewer than twenty plants in all in an industry, its total number of plants is shown in parentheses, and the average size relative refers to the average size of that number of plants. In the table, the 34 industries have been arranged in order of the degree of twenty-plant concentration in the United States.

TABLE 3–2

Average Numbers of Employees in the Largest Twenty Plants in Thirty-four Industries in Eight Countries, Expressed as Relatives to the Average Numbers of Employees of the Largest Twenty Plants in the Same Industries in the United States[a]

Industries	United States	United Kingdom	Sweden	Canada	France	Japan	Italy	India
			RELATIVE AVERAGE SIZE OF THE TWENTY LARGEST PLANTS[a]					
High to moderate plant concentration								
Explosives	100	118	17 (13)	n.a.	62	26	23	n.a.
Electric light bulbs	100	54	n.a.	n.a.	49	34	33	n.a.
Plastics	100	64	9	n.a.	n.a.	n.a.	13	12
Distilled liquor	100	22	6	n.a.	38	50	22	n.a.
Sugar refining	100	90	17 (16)	n.a.	11	39	41	24
Shipbuilding	100	131	40	n.a.	89	155	60	42
Drugs	100	56	3 (18)	n.a.	17	18	26	n.a.
Steel works and rolling mills	100	38	13	5	44	19	8	18
Agricultural machinery	100	n.a.[b]	n.a.	n.a.	25	12	12	n.a.
Aircraft	100	29	n.a.	11	10	n.a.	2	2
Nonferrous metals	100	181	22 (18)	117	46	155	70	29
Tobacco products	100	79	8 (8)	23	23	n.a.	60	78
Petroleum refining	100	28 (18)	11 (5)	14	29	15	12	9 (10)
Breweries	100	54	7	n.a.	15	28 (13)	11	2
Soap	100	99	9	n.a.	31	42	24	40
Motor vehicles and parts	100	48	n.a.	17 (16)	40	18	25	10
Rubber products	100	61	9	23	43	34	35	29

Moderate to low plant
concentration

Pulp mills	100	n.a.	69	160	45	70	n.a.	n.a.
Hardware	100	82	n.a.	n.a.	15	12	19	n.a.
Glass products	100	86	10	n.a.	30	40	27	31
Seafood (canned, packaged, cured)	100	36	20	66	39	109	31	n.a.
Cement	100	79	42 (8)	n.a.	81	130	69	n.a.
Leather tanning	100	66	19	n.a.	72	31	54	36
Wool textiles	100	113	32	n.a.	142	158	178	64
Cotton textiles	100	24	n.a.	n.a.	n.a.	17	57	n.a.
Paper and paperboard	100	90	43	n.a.	34	79	55	57
Paints and varnishes	100	110	10	n.a.	35	35	24	39
Canned and preserved fruits, vegetables	100	77	8	25	19	17	15	8
Wood containers	100	60	10	n.a.	n.a.	28	38	n.a.
Grain products	100	91	11	36	62	34	32	41
Knitting mills	100	97	19	n.a.	70	33	41	12
Electrical industrial machinery	100	129	n.a.	54	66	77	n.a.	n.a.
Sawmills and planing mills	100	49	30	53	38	20	20	19
Apparel	100	100	17	32	44	29	36	5

ᵃWhere the number of plants in an industry is less than 20, the actual number is shown in parentheses, and the size relative refers to the average size of that number of plants.

ᵇNot available.

Sources: Appendix Tables A–1 to A–8. Calculated (see text).

Table 3–2 should be substantially self-explanatory. It is clear that in the seven countries other than the United States the larger plants in their industries generally tend to be significantly smaller in absolute size than the larger plants in counterpart industries in the United States. This tendency, however, is of varying strength among countries, within any country varies in strength among industries, and for all countries is more marked for some industries than for others. Moreover the tendency is reversed in the case of a small minority of industries in most countries. In the United Kingdom there are six industries, in Japan five, in Canada two, and in France and Italy each one, in which the estimated average sizes of the largest twenty plants exceed those of the counterpart industries in the United States. The United States lags in average plant size most notably in woolen textiles, shipbuilding, and nonferrous metals. The plant size findings in the last category, however, are of questionable meaning, because the two-digit nonferrous metals industry comprehends several individual industries—aluminum, copper, lead, and zinc in particular—and the composition of the nonferrous metals category by such industries evidently varies considerably among countries. In general, however, judging from the 34 industries sampled, the United States sweeps the board in the matter of average absolute size of its larger manufacturing plants.

The detailed information contained in Table 3–2 may be summarized in Table 3–3 by tabulating for each country the median plant-size relative for the industries for which it is represented, the range of all plant-size relatives excluding the largest and the smallest for the country, the approximate quartile plant-size relatives, and the percentage of industry plant-size relatives which are 70 or above.

Table 3–3 shows that in the matter of manufacturing-plant sizes, only the United Kingdom of the countries studied comes reasonably close to the United States, and that on the average the other six countries tend to have in their

TABLE 3–3

Summary of Findings in Table 3–2 concerning Average Sizes of the
Twenty Largest Plants in Thirty-four Industries, Expressed as Relatives

Country	Number of Industries Covered	Median Plant-Size Relative	Range of Relatives, excluding Largest and Smallest Relative	Quartile Relatives (approximate)	Percentage of Industries with Plant-Size Relative of 70 or above
United States	(34)	100	100–100	100–100	100%
United Kingdom	(32)	78	24–131	52– 98	53%
France	(31)	39	11– 89	24– 63	19%
Japan	(31)	34	12–155	19– 71	26%
Italy	(32)	29	8– 70	19– 48	6%
Canada	(14)	28	5–117	16– 53	14%
India	(22)	26	2– 64	10– 40	5%
Sweden	(27)	13	6– 43	9– 24	0%

Source: Table 3–2.

industries larger plants of much smaller size than are found in the United States. Despite the possible unreliability of findings for a few industries, this overall conclusion seems well supported. Given the ranking of countries in Table 3–3 in terms of the value of the median plant-size relative, it is notable that Japan and to a lesser extent Canada display a much wider dispersion of plant-size relatives than the other countries. Though on the average having its larger manufacturing plants with an average size about one-third of that in the United States, Japan has five industries with larger average plant size than the counterpart industries in the United States, and in 26 per cent of Japanese industries counted, the average plant size was 70 per cent or more of the corresponding size in the United States. France and Italy, on the other hand, have a more consistent tendency toward smaller plant sizes than those found in the United States. India has plant-size relatives below 100 throughout, and substantially below in nearly all cases. Sweden, somewhat surprisingly, has the smallest plants of all eight countries according to every measure.

The average size of larger manufacturing plants seems to be related in a complex way to the degree of industrialization of countries, to the size of their populations, and to their geography. Not all of these factors however would seem to "explain" the differences in plant size observed; it is not clear for example that the fact that Sweden has a small population (while being rather highly industrialized) should lead it to develop its industry in a multiplicity of rather small-scale individual plants. A variety of institutional and other factors evidently contributes to the explanation of the observed pattern of intercountry differences in the sizes of principal manufacturing plants. We will comment on possible explanations of plant-size differences in the concluding chapter of this study.

All the preceding findings of course refer to the estimated average sizes of the largest twenty plants in the sample of manufacturing industries in the eight countries under study. Is the picture much altered if we refer instead to the average sizes of smaller absolute numbers of plants, such as the largest four or eight plants? Our detailed calculations of the estimated average sizes of the largest four and eight plants for the same industries indicate that the general comparative showing is not significantly altered, although the average plant size in the United States, and to a lesser degree in the United Kingdom, appears relatively somewhat larger when the largest four or eight plants are referred to. Consistently, intercountry differences in plant size appear somewhat smaller if the average size of the largest fifty plants in each industry is taken as a measure. It is our view, however, that the preceding comparisons of the average sizes of the largest twenty plants in various industries in the eight countries fairly well represent the general tendencies in intercountry differentials in the sizes of manufacturing plants.

The preceding plant-size measures are all of course in terms of plant employment, as distinct from capacity or output. The use of employment as a proxy variable to measure plant size has been, as noted above, not one of choice but of necessity, since for most countries the censuses of manufactures measure plant size only in terms of number of workers. Use of employment as a size measure may result in significantly different comparative showings for different countries than would have been found had plant capacity or output been used as a measure of plant size. Employment is a less than fully satisfactory measure of plant capacity so far as it is influenced by differences in technology, capital intensity in production, worker productivity, length of work day and week, and rate of utilization of plant—as well as by plant capacity. Intercountry differences in these combined respects however are generally of such a character as to lead to an understatement of relative plant size (as measured by capacity) in the United States as compared to other countries in general, and in the Western European countries as compared to those of the Far East. This is because there is evidently a moderate tendency in the Western European countries, and a somewhat stronger one in the Far Eastern countries, toward higher labor intensity (lower capital intensity) in production, and toward lower productivity per worker, than found in the United States, as well as some average tendency to lag in technology behind the United States. In addition, there is a significant incidence of "nominal" employment in the Far East. These tendencies would appear to offset more than fully any contrary tendency to secure greater output per employee through longer work days or weeks abroad.

COMPARATIVE PLANT CONCENTRATION

In devising measures of plant concentration, we have calculated for each of the industries listed in Tables 3–1 and 3–2, for each country, estimates of the percentages of all industry workers controlled by the largest four, eight, twenty, and fifty plants, employing the same estimating procedures previously described.[4] A fairly full profile of comparative plant concentration might then be presented, but it would involve the presentation of a complex jumble of a very large quantity of numbers. After comparing all of our findings, we have concluded that a good rough notion of comparative plant concentration can be gained from examining only the findings referring to percentage of industry employment accounted for by the largest twenty plants in each industry in each country. In presenting data on comparative plant concentration as measured by percentage of industry employment by the largest twenty plants in an industry, we will follow the same procedure used in presenting data on comparative plant sizes above, reducing all plant concentration ratios to relatives, with the relative for each industry for each country other than the United States rep-

4. See above, pp. 26 to 30.

resenting the relationship of the twenty-plant concentration ratio for that industry to the twenty-plant concentration ratio for the same industry in the United States.

Thus for any single industry, such as the canned and preserved fruits and vegetables industry shown below, we have proceeded from estimated concentration ratios to relatives as indicated:

Country	Estimated Percentage of Workers Employed by the Twenty Largest Plants	Estimated Comparative Size of Twenty-Plant Concentration Ratios
United States	17.8	100
United Kingdom	37.2	209
Sweden	44.4	249
Canada	37.7	212
France	23.3	131
Japan	17.8	100
Italy	20.4	115
India	80.1	450

Table 3–4 presents plant-concentration relatives derived from estimated twenty-plant concentration ratios for 34 industries for the eight countries. The industries are arrayed in decreasing order of plant concentration in the United States. Industries designated as having high-to-moderate plant concentration ratios have twenty-plant ratios of from 85.9 to 33.4 in the United States; those designated as having moderate-to-low plant concentration have corresponding ratios of from 29.4 to 2.9. The findings must be generally viewed as providing only rough indicators of comparative concentration, since the individual estimates are subject to the possibly significant estimating error, and tests of United States estimates against precise plant-concentration measures suggest there are appreciable errors in the case of about half the industries, although overestimates and underestimates occur with about equal frequency.

TABLE 3–4

Comparative Twenty-Plant Concentration in Thirty-four Industries in Eight Countries, as Measured in Terms of Relatives to Twenty-Plant Concentration in the United States for Matching Industries

Industries	United States	United Kingdom	Sweden	Canada	France	Japan	Italy	India
			RELATIVE TWENTY-PLANT CONCENTRATION[a]					
High to moderate plant concentration								
Explosives	100	94	116 (13)	n.a.	76	111	100	n.a.
Electric light bulbs	100	77	n.a.	n.a.	114	64	111	n.a.
Plastics	100	120	108	n.a.	n.a.	n.a.	125	70
Distilled liquor	100	95	101	n.a.	62	56	31	n.a.
Sugar refining	100	145	185 (16)	n.a.	86	127	108	46
Shipbuilding	100	75	186	n.a.	129	134	188	186
Drugs	100	104	211 (18)	n.a.	46	34	83	n.a.
Steel works and rolling mills	100	85	189	68	125	160	153	92
Agricultural machinery	100	n.a.[b]	n.a.	n.a.	106	56	109	n.a.
Aircraft	100	100	n.a.	217	127	n.a.	230	220
Nonferrous metals	100	86	233 (18)	179	153	76	148	228
Tobacco products	100	181	234 (8)	225	218	n.a.	113	31
Petroleum refining	100	234 (18)	234 (5)	188	218	218	210	234 (10)
Breweries	100	66	107	n.a.	72	249 (13)	204	24
Soap	100	207	198	n.a.	176	138	63	192
Motor vehicles and parts	100	102	n.a.	294 (16)	160	87	230	101
Rubber products	100	142	294	252	176	95	224	232

Moderate to low plant concentration

Pulp mills	100	n.a.	192	160	152	265	n.a.	n.a.
Hardware	100	49	n.a.	n.a.	89	32	115	n.a.
Glass products	100	178	227	n.a.	87	109	105	173
Seafood (canned, preserved, cured)	100	156	229	146	78	21	210	n.a.
Cement	100	248	398 (8)	n.a.	133	278	111	n.a.
Leather tanning	100	91	380	n.a.	112	132	127	78
Wool textiles	100	50	301	n.a.	88	104	124	340
Cotton textiles	100	67	n.a.	n.a.	n.a.	25	124	n.a.
Paper and paperboard	100	161	285	n.a.	170	135	192	329
Paints and varnishes	100	193	400	n.a.	154	261	198	366
Canned and preserved fruits, vegetables	100	209	249	212	131	100	115	450
Wood containers	100	118	514	n.a.	n.a.	33	100	n.a.
Grain products	100	282	876	360	178	110	55	54
Knitting mills	100	175	470	n.a.	172	92	120	244
Electrical industrial machinery	100	323	n.a.	518	305	298	n.a.	n.a.
Sawmills and planing mills	100	157	370	340	108	24	197	500
Apparel	100	227	722	417	135	176	86	159

[a]Where the number of plants in an industry is less than 20, the actual number is shown in parentheses, and the concentration relative refers to the ratio of 100 per cent (controlled by the actual number of plants) to the corresponding percentage of United States employment in the industry controlled by the largest 20 plants.
[b]Not available.

Sources: Appendix Tables A–1 to A–8. Calculated (see text).

A reading of Table 3–4 suggests that there is a central tendency for the seven countries other than the United States to have from moderately to substantially higher degrees of plant concentration in the industries sampled—as indicated by the fact that on the average the twenty largest plants in their various industries account for larger proportions of industry employment—but that around this central tendency there is in every country a wide dispersion in relative plant concentration for individual industries. The further interpretation of Table 3–4 is facilitated by summarizing its findings in Table 3–5, which shows for each country the median plant-concentration relative for its array of industries, the range of its plant-concentration relatives as determined after omitting the largest and smallest relative, and the approximate plant-concentration relatives at the first and third quartiles of its array.

Table 3–5 confirms the finding that the central tendency in each country is toward higher plant concentration within individual industries, but shows that this tendency is especially marked in only three countries—India, Canada, and Sweden. In Japan, Italy, France, and the United Kingdom, the central tendency is toward plant concentration only slightly or moderately greater than that found in the United States. Around these central tendencies, however, there is a marked dispersion evidenced by the wide range and interquartile range of plant-concentration relatives for individual industries, as shown in the last two columns of Table 3–5. This dispersion is proportionately somewhat greater than the corresponding dispersion in relative absolute sizes of larger plants, shown in Table 3–3 above.

One reflection of this dispersion is the fact that the five largest countries outside the United States have the following percentages of the number of their industries (in the sample) with *lower* plant concentration than found in corresponding industries in the United States: Japan, 42 per cent; Italy, 16 per cent; France, 29 per cent; United Kingdom,

TABLE 3-5

Summary of Findings in Table 3-4 concerning Twenty-Plant Concentration
in Thirty-four Industries, Expressed as Relatives

Country	Number of Industries Covered	Median Plant-Concentration Relative	Range of Relatives excluding Largest and Smallest Relative	Quartile Relatives (approximate)
United States	(34)	100	100–100	100–100
Japan	(31)	109	24–278	56–160
Italy	(32)	122	55–230	106–194
France	(31)	129	62–218	88–170
United Kingdom	(32)	131	50–282	88–178
India	(22)	189	31–450	76–256
Canada	(14)	221	146–417	170–350
Sweden	(27)	234	107–722	90–380

Source: Table 3-4.

34 per cent, India, 32 per cent. (This showing of course reflects dually the large dispersions in relative plant concentration among industries and the relatively small excesses in median plant concentration over that found in the United States.) At the other extreme, the percentages of the number of their industries that had plant-concentration relatives above 200 (had double or more the plant concentration found in the United States) were as follows for the same countries: Japan, 19 per cent; Italy, 19 per cent; France, 10 per cent; United Kingdom, 21 per cent; India, 41 per cent. (The corresponding percentages for Canada and Sweden are 64 and 67.) In the matter of comparative plant concentration, where each country is viewed as a unit, the variance is such as almost to overwhelm the central tendency in all the countries except Canada and Sweden, and even there the variance is quite large. For numerous individual industries, however, there are of course very distinct intercountry differences in the degree of plant concentration, and for a majority of the industries in each country outside the United States, plant concentration is from slightly to very substantially higher, although in only 8 of the 34 industries does the United States have a lower plant concentration than every other country.

The finding of "on-the-general-average" somewhat higher plant concentration by industries outside the United States, with wide dispersions around this central tendency, is of course coupled with the finding (see Tables 3–2 and 3–3) of on-the-average substantially lower absolute average plant size in the same countries, where reference in both cases is to the largest twenty plants in each industry. Were it not for the latter tendency, plant concentration in countries outside the United States would be much greater than it is. The combined findings suggest that in a broad average way there is a positive association between the absolute sizes of plants in an industry in a country and the size of the entire industry in the country (small industries, smaller plants),

48

TABLE 3-6

Comparison of Plant-Size Relatives and Plant-Concentration Relatives for Thirty-four Industries, for Twenty Plants in Each Industry

Country	Median Relatives		Upper-Quartile Relatives		Lower-Quartile Relatives	
	Size	Concentration	Size	Concentration	Size	Concentration
United States	100	100	100	100	100	100
United Kingdom	78	131	98	178	52	88
France	39	129	63	170	24	88
Japan	34	109	71	160	19	56
Italy	29	122	48	194	19	106
Canada	28	221	53	350	16	170
India	26	189	40	256	10	76
Sweden	13	234	24	380	9	90

Sources: Tables 3-3 and 3-5.

though not a sufficiently strong association to forestall fully on-the-average higher plant concentration in countries with smaller industries. Moreover this association is far from reflecting any regular functional relationship, with the result that there is practically no correlation between plant-size relatives and plant-concentration relatives in general inter-country comparisons or in individual industry comparisons —generally because of the highly variable relationship of the absolute size of the largest twenty plants in the individual industry to size of the industry.

This low degree of association between comparative plant size and comparative plant concentration is suggested in Table 3–6, which compares countries in terms of their median relatives and upper and lower quartile relatives showing comparative plant size and comparative plant concentration, as measured at the twenty-plant level. It is more strongly suggested in Table 3–7, which compares relative plant size and relative plant concentration for ten selected industries (chosen for neatness of definition) in the United Kingdom and in Italy. It will be noted that within either country, there is substantially no correlation between plant-size relatives and plant-concentration relatives for individual industries.

Further, the two-country comparison reveals that in six out of ten industries Italy has smaller average plant sizes but a higher degree of plant concentration, and that in two of the remaining four cases in which Italy has both lower plant size and lower plant concentration, the intercountry difference in plant size is far from proportional to the intercountry difference in plant concentration. The same impression is sustained by further such comparisons based on Tables 3–2 and 3–4. The generally low degree of association of comparative plant size with comparative plant concentration is attributable to the ubiquitous random variability, among countries for the same industry, of the proportionate importance of the largest twenty plants.

TABLE 3–7

Comparison of Plant-Size Relatives and Plant-Concentration
Relatives for the United Kingdom and Italy, for Ten Industries

| | United Kingdom | | | Italy |
Industries	Size Relative	Concentration Relative	Size Relative	Concentration Relative
Shipbuilding	131	75	60	188
Explosives	118	94	23	100
Soap	99	207	24	63
Paper and paperboard	90	161	55	192
Sugar refining	90	145	41	108
Cement	79	248	69	111
Plastics	64	120	13	125
Canned and preserved fruits, vegetables	60	209	38	115
Electric light bulbs	54	77	33	111
Steel works and rolling mills	38	85	8	153

Sources: Tables 3–2 and 3–4.

The foregoing analysis of comparative plant concentration
in the eight countries under examination is strictly comparative, since it rests on measures of twenty-plant concentration
expressed entirely as relatives to concentration in the United
States industries, with the degree of plant concentration in
the United States for every industry being assigned a relative
value of 100. It should be useful to supplement this analysis
with some tabulation of information which reveals the absolute degrees of plant concentration in the various industries
in the several countries. The single most useful tabulation of
the several we have compiled shows for each country for each
industry the minimum number of plants required to account
for 50 per cent of total employment in the industry. This
number in each case is an estimate, representing the arithmetic mean of statistically possible largest and smallest minimum number of plants, as calculated from frequency distributions shown in Appendix Tables A–1 through A–8. The

TABLE 3–8

Number of Largest Plants Accounting for 50 Per Cent of Industry Employment, for Twenty-four Industries in Eight Countries

Industries	United States	United Kingdom	Sweden	Canada	France	Japan	Italy	India
	NUMBER OF PLANTS TO ACCOUNT FOR 50 PER CENT OF INDUSTRY EMPLOYMENT							
Electric light bulbs	7	17	n.a.ᵃ	n.a.	7	26	5	n.a.
Explosives	8	11	2	n.a.	13	4	1	n.a.
Plastics	11	9	9	n.a.	n.a.	n.a.	4	24
Distilled liquor	12	14	9	n.a.	36	38	125	n.a.
Sugar refining	18	12	5	n.a.	25	11	22	5,400
Shipbuilding	19	31	4	n.a.	11	10	5	5
Petroleum refining	24	4	1	8	8	7	3	1
Drugs	24	21	3	n.a.	93	60	33	n.a.
Breweries	29	67	26	n.a.	46	4	8	52
Steel works and rolling mills	31	29	6	44	16	11	7	25
Aircraft	35	20	n.a.	4	17	n.a.	1	2
Soap	35	6	6	n.a.	9	11	107	5
Pulp mills	43	n.a.	16	26	13	11	n.a.	n.a.
Cement	58	16	3	n.a.	37	13	51	n.a.

Leather tanning	62	74	4	n.a.	69	60	52	96
Seafood (canned, preserved, cured)	64	47	16	35	64	2,476	16	n.a.
Wool textiles	91	247	11	n.a.	106	74	61	6
Paper and paperboard	96	31	16	n.a.	37	65	33	7
Grain products	107	53	5	45	237	406	3,236	6,550
Paints and varnishes	114	36	8	n.a.	57	21	20	7
Wood containers	128	130	9	n.a.	n.a.	2,290	718	n.a.
Canned and preserved fruits, vegetables	182	94	26	38	71	113	40	5
Knitting mills	292	117	23	n.a.	127	770	327	79
Sawmills, planing mills	1,072	401	121	299	939	5,664	525	43,210

aNot available.

Sources: Appendix Tables A–1 to A–8. Calculated (see text).

tabulation is presented in Table 3–8, and covers 24 of the 34 industries sampled, 8 being omitted because of broad industry definition and 2 because of small country coverage.

Subject to a general caveat concerning probable errors in the estimates tabulated, several conclusions may be drawn from Table 3–8. First, a significantly high degree of plant concentration, in the sense that a rather small absolute number of plants (let us say fifteen or less) control half the employment in an industry, is present in a distinct minority of industries sampled in six countries: in 4 of 24 industries in the United States, in 6 of 23 in the United Kingdom, in 6 of 22 in France, in 7 of 22 in Japan, in 8 of 23 in Italy, and in 2 of 8 in Canada. There is a heavy incidence of high plant concentration in Sweden, a circumstance explained by the small size of the country and its industries, and to a somewhat lesser extent in India. Plant concentration in the remaining industries in all countries is from moderate to very low. Second, as regards comparative concentration, there are only seven industries in which the United States has lower plant concentration than every one of the other seven countries— petroleum refining, aircraft, pulp mills, cement, paper and paperboard, paints and varnishes, and canned and preserved fruits and vegetables. However the industries sampled are in the United States on the average less concentrated than those of comparable industries in the other countries, and are much more frequently less concentrated than they are more concentrated. From Table 3–8, 136 separate comparisons can be made of a United States industry with a counterpart industry in another of the seven foreign countries. A summary of these comparisons shows that in approximately 60 per cent of the comparisons (81) the United States industry has substantially lower plant concentration than the foreign industry, that in about 19 per cent of the comparisons (26) the United States has substantially higher plant concentration than the foreign industry, and that in the remaining 21 per cent of comparisons (29) the difference in plant concentration between the United States industry and the foreign industry is either relatively slight or negligible. This general order of comparison applies roughly to individual countries with three exceptions. Sweden has higher plant concentration than the United States in all industries counted, and much higher in 19 of 22 cases. Japan and India are more strongly represented than the other countries with industries of much lower plant concentration than corresponding industries in the United States, and are very lightly represented by industries with roughly the same concentration in the United States.

In general, there would appear to exist on the average in the seven countries other than the United States a technical basis for somewhat higher concentration of control of industries by relatively few firms.[5] Such a base exists for a majority of industries in all of these countries, for a strong majority of industries in Canada, Italy, and India, and for all industries sampled in Sweden. However a strong technical basis for high concentration of control by firms seems to be uncommon in the United States, and a stronger basis in other countries is frequently not strong in absolute terms.

COMPARATIVE PLANT EFFICIENCY

The comparisons presented above of the sizes of the largest plants in different industries in the several countries, which revealed substantial intercountry differences with respect to plant size, naturally suggest the following question. To what extent do countries have differences with respect to efficiency in manufacturing production, so far as efficiency is affected by the absolute scale of plant?

In each of the industries studied, there is presumably some minimum optimal scale of plant (i.e. the smallest scale at

5. See above, p. 25 n., for comment on the meaning of "technical basis" for company concentration.

which minimum costs of production may be attained), and a certain incidence of diseconomies or higher costs at successively smaller scales of plant, as registered in a function relating average cost of production to scale of plant. In some industries, unit costs will rise sharply as plant scale is reduced appreciably below minimum optimal scale; in others, the rise in costs is slight until the plant has been reduced in size to a minor fraction of minimum optimal scale.[6] The relative efficiency of production in any industry, so far as efficiency is determined by plant scale (but only so far), may be measured by the percentage of industry output which is produced by plants of reasonably efficient scale—i.e. by plants as large or larger than minimum optimal scale, or by smaller plants which experience only slight diseconomies of small scale and have net costs no more than, let us say, three or four per cent above the minimum obtainable.

If the percentage of industry output supplied by plants of reasonably efficient scale were taken as a measure of efficiency for each industry in the several countries, it should be possible to use a tabulation of such percentages for each industry for all countries to determine the comparative efficiency in manufacturing production of the various countries, so far as efficiency is determined by plant scale. And it would be convenient to present just such a table, if we had the data to support it. The data we lack are those referring to the output or capacity of plants for any of the countries outside the United States, and those measuring the minimum optimal scale of plant and the shape of the plant scale curve short of this optimum for most of the industries studied—in general or for the individual countries in the event that optimal plant scales for a given industry differ among countries. Thus, we cannot approach an analysis of comparative effi-

6. See Joe S. Bain, *Barriers to New Competition* (Cambridge, Mass., 1956), pp. 68 to 85, for findings referring to American manufacturing industries.

ciency among countries as determined by plant sizes in a direct fashion.

We can however, by employing a few heroic assumptions and some findings from another study, produce some very crude estimates of possible or probable differences in plant efficiency among countries. The first assumption is based on findings of a previous study by this writer[7] to the effect that in a sample of twenty manufacturing industries in the United States, the proportion of total industry output supplied by plants of reasonably efficient scale[8] lay uniformly between 70 and 90 per cent. (This study happened to cover seven of the industries examined here.) Our first assumption is that this tendency is found throughout manufacturing industries in the United States, and in particular that in each industry in this country at least 70 per cent of industry output is produced by plants of reasonably efficient scale. A second assumption is that the number of workers in a plant is a sufficiently good proxy measure of scale within any particular industry, that it is also true that at least 70 per cent of the employees in each of the industries in the United States are employed in plants of reasonably efficient scale. This assumption, which is probably not very erroneous, is necessary if we are to proceed with an analysis of plant sizes measured entirely in terms of number of employees.

Given these two assumptions, we can determine from available data, as detailed in Appendix Table A–1, the smallest size class of plant in each industry in the United States which must be included to account for 70 per cent of the employees in the industry. For the soap industry in 1954, for example,

7. Ibid., pp. 184–87.
8. That is, either of optimal scale (minimum optimal scale or larger, in a context wherein larger scales are found to be no less efficient), or of suboptimal scale such that, the slope of the scale curve at scales smaller than minimum optimal being taken into account, unit costs of production did not exceed the minimum attainable by more than 3 or 4 per cent.

the Census of Manufactures shows the following percentage distribution of employees by size classes of plants, size being measured by number of employees:

Plant Size as Measured by Number of Employees	Percentages of Industry Employees in Each Size Class
1,000 and over	21.2
500 to 999	12.3
250 to 499	21.7
100 to 249	8.1
50 to 99	12.2
20 to 49	10.1
1 to 19	14.4
Total	100.0

It is evident that in order to account for 70 per cent of the workers in the soap industry, we must include plants with between 50 and 99 employees each (only 63.3 per cent are included in plants with more than 100 employees each). Such a size class in each industry in the United States is assumed to be the smallest reasonably efficient size class, and in particular the lower limit of this size class (the smallest tapped to account for 70 per cent of the employees in the industry) is assumed to be the smallest plant size, as measured in terms of number of employees, which is reasonably efficient in the industry in question. (This, our third assumption, tends in general to give a conservatively low estimate of minimum size for a reasonably efficient plant.)

The fourth assumption is to the effect that in each particular industry the minimum scale (in terms of number of employees) of a plant of reasonably efficient size is the same for all countries, or that in the other seven countries it is the same as it is in the United States. This assumption may be questioned on the grounds (1) that intercountry differences in technology lead to corresponding differences in efficient plant scales in various industries, with lagging technologies outside the United States being associated with smaller minimum optimal plant scales; (2) that differences among countries with respect to relative factor prices, featuring outside the United States higher relative prices for capital goods as compared to those for labor, may establish smaller scales as optimal where relative capital goods prices are higher; and (3) that in countries with smaller markets than those of the United States, and geographically dispersed population, smaller, geographically dispersed plants may be in the net more efficient if delivery costs are taken into account.

Our feelings on these points may be summarized as follows. As regards intercountry differences in technology possibly supporting smaller plant scales as optimal outside the United States, it appears that wide intercountry variations in technology are uncommon, technology being an exportable and widely exported commodity. Moreover, suppose that foreign technologies do lag in some industries, making smaller plant scales optimal given these technologies but less efficient than larger scales would be with improved technologies. Then if the technological lag is attributable to lassitude or comparable factors rather than to high capital goods prices or capital shortage, the pseudo-optimal plant scales linked with inferior technologies are in fact suboptimal and should be counted as such. Regarding the possibility that higher relative capital goods prices will tend to make smaller plants optimal (as well as inducing more labor-intensive production), this hypothesis is a strong one only if relative capital goods prices abroad are sufficiently higher that they "price out of the market" the use of specialized types of capital equipment on the use of which considerable economies of large-scale plants are based in the United States. This is a possibility, and we have no systematic evidence which would reveal its importance. But on the basis of surveys of technologies and methods of production in various industries at home and abroad, we feel that the tendency in question would at most have a scattered incidence among the industries sampled. Finally as regards the effects of thin and geographically dispersed markets on optimal plant scales, the evidence on the number of plants and on the size and geographical dispersion of population in the countries studied outside the United States does not suggest that otherwise suboptimal plant scales are *generally* justified in these countries as "efficient" once delivery costs are accounted for. However an exception may be made to this generalization for *some* industries in Canada and possibly a few in Sweden.

In sum, therefore, we are willing to adopt, subject to some reservations and qualifications, the tentative assumption that the minimum size of a plant of reasonably efficient size in the bulk of industries is about the same in the other seven countries as it is in the United States. In making the assumption with specific reference to plant scales as measured by number of employees, we are protected in a degree by the fact that higher labor intensity in production in foreign countries as it occurs produces an upward bias in plant-size measures in these countries, and thus biases comparative measures of efficiency in the direction of exaggerating the comparative efficiency of plants in countries outside the United States.

Adopting the fourth assumption, it is possible to derive an estimate for each industry in each foreign country of its comparative efficiency in plant size by measuring the percentage of industry employees which are employed in plants of a size no smaller than the lower size limit of the lowest plant-size class tapped in the United States to account for 70 per cent of the United States employment in the same industry. Thus, in the soap industry, the percentage distribution of workers by plant-size classes is as follows in Italy:

Comparative Plant Size and Concentration

Plant Size as Measured by Number of Employees	Percentages of Industry Employees in Each Size Class
500 to 1,000	3.0
100 to 499	27.1
50 to 99	13.6
10 to 49	25.2
1 to 9	31.1
Total	100.0

In the United States soap industry, the smallest size for a reasonably efficient plant has been established at 50 employees in the table preceding this one. In Italy, 43.7 per cent of employees in the soap industry are employed in plants employing 50 or more workers. Following our assumptions, we conclude that only 43.7 per cent of Italian soap industry employees work in plants of reasonably efficient size.

The procedure just exemplified has been employed to calculate the percentage of workers employed in plants of reasonably efficient size in each of 24 industries (the same list shown in Table 3–8, omitting 8 industries of unduly broad definition and 2 with poor country coverage). In this calculation, the percentage for each industry in the United States is by assumption 70 (more properly 70 plus). In the other countries, any percentages found by this procedure to be above 70 are written as 70 to minimize the error inherent in including all plants within a size class down to its lower limit, when the 70 per cent level in the United States is most frequently reached somewhere above the lower limit of the critical size class. Our procedures, assumptions, and data do not permit us to estimate meaningfully percentages of industry employment in reasonably efficient plants above 70 per cent.

The preceding serves to explain the meaning of the data presented in Table 3–9, and the severe limitations on the

TABLE 3-9

Percentages of Workers Employed in Plants of Reasonably Efficient Size in Twenty-four Industries in Eight Countries

Industries	United States	United Kingdom	Sweden	Canada	France	Japan	Italy	India
	PERCENTAGE OF WORKERS IN THE INDUSTRY							
Electric light bulbs	70	49	n.a.ª	n.a.	65	28	59	n.a.
Explosives	70	70	53	n.a.	62	50	58	n.a.
Plastics	70	70	25	n.a.	n.a.	n.a.	40	20
Distilled liquor	70	n.a.	18	n.a.	29	34	14	n.a.
Sugar refining	70	70	34	n.a.	70	61	70	70
Shipbuilding	70	70	70	n.a.	70	70	70	70
Petroleum refining	70	70	56	40	70	66	58	70
Drugs	70	69	28	n.a.	24	45	51	n.a.
Breweries	70	54	11	n.a.	23	70	46	21
Steel works and rolling mills	70	70	70	0	70	70	44	36
Aircraft	70	70	n.a.	63	53	53	52	0
Soap	70	70	61	n.a.	70	70	44	70
Pulp mills	70	n.a.	70	70	70	55	n.a.	n.a.
Cement	70	70	64	n.a.	51	70	44	n.a.

Leather tanning	70	54	66	n.a.	47	26	41	34
Seafood (canned, preserved, cured)	70	45	46	67	70	26	51	n.a.
Wool textiles	70	51	61	n.a.	56	55	67	60
Paper and paperboard	70	70	70	n.a.	54	52	50	70
Grain products	70	70	69	49	38	27	15	52
Paints and varnishes	70	70	59	n.a.	53	65	52	64
Wood containers	70	54	34	n.a.	n.a.	68	14	n.a.
Canned and preserved fruits, vegetables	70	70	56	70	67	49	52	70
Knitting mills	70	70	52	n.a.	45	17	34	14
Sawmills and planing mills	70	70	68	59	58	42	52	70

Sources: Appendix Tables A–1 to A–8. Calculated (see text).

accuracy and interpretation of them. They at best represent rough guesses at comparative efficiency as determined by plant size, subject to numerous qualifications. The overall showing concerning comparative industrial efficiency as determined by size of plant may be summarized in Table 3–10, which presents for each of the seven countries outside the United States (1) the percentage of the number of industries counted in which the proportion of total industry employees working in plants of reasonably efficient size is estimated to be less than 70 per cent (percentage of industries with "substandard" efficiency in plant scale), and (2) the arithmetic mean, *for substandard industries,* of the percentages of workers employed in plants of reasonably efficient scale.

TABLE 3–10

Summary of Findings in Table 3–9 concerning
Comparative Incidence of Inefficiently Small Plants
in Twenty-four Industries in Seven Countries

Country	Number of Industries Counted	Percentage of Number of Industries in Which Less than 70 Per Cent of Employees Work in Reasonably Efficient Plants	Mean Percentage of Employees Working in Reasonably Efficient Plants, for Industries in Which Percentage is Less than 70 Per Cent
United Kingdom	(22)	32	54
Sweden	(22)	82	48
Canada	(8)	75	46
France	(20)	75	48
Japan	(23)	78	46
Italy	(23)	91	42
India	(16)	56	33

Source: Table 3–9.

Table 3–10 suggests some very interesting tendencies in intercountry differences in efficiency in plant scale in manufacturing. Assuming that 70 per cent of industry employees work in plants of reasonably efficient scale in each industry in the United States, deriving a standard range of reasonably efficient plant scales for each industry accordingly from Census of Manufactures data for the United States, and testing plant scales in each industry in the other seven countries against this standard, it appears that there is a high incidence among industries of inefficiently small plants in all of the other seven countries excepting the United Kingdom. In that country, in only about 30 per cent of the number of industries sampled were fewer than 70 per cent of industry employees working in plants of reasonably efficient scale, and in the 30 per cent of "inefficient" industries, the mean proportion of workers employed in reasonably efficient plants was 54 per cent. In Sweden, Canada, France, Japan, and Italy, the proportion of the number of industries with fewer than 70 per cent of industry employees working in plants of reasonably efficient scale ranged from 75 to 91 per cent, with the proportion of "inefficient" industries being highest in Italy and Sweden, and next highest in Japan. Thus in these countries, in from three-fourths to over four-fifths of the industries more than 30 per cent of employees worked in plants of inefficiently small scale. In these five countries moreover, in the high proportion of industries with relatively inefficient plant organization, the mean percentage of employees working in plants of reasonably efficient scale ranged from 42 to 48 per cent, so that on the average, excluding the minor fraction of industries in which plant scales were relatively efficient, less than half of manufacturing employees worked in plants of reasonably efficient scale. In India the proportion of industries with serious inefficiencies of plant scale was smaller, at 56 per cent, but in these industries the mean proportion of workers employed in plants of reasonably efficient scale was only 33 per cent.

The magnitude of the inefficiencies incurred in inefficiently small plants, as measured for example by the percentage by which production costs are elevated above the lowest

attainable, is not estimated; but the character of our definitions and procedures is such that the average elevation of
cost should generally be 5 per cent or greater in all cases,[9]
and might be substantially greater in at least a minority of
the industries in question.

The preceding findings, in view of the several rough-and-
ready assumptions on which they are based, should of course
not be viewed as quantitatively accurate. On the other hand,
they would appear to have a fair chance of being qualita-
tively correct, and should not necessarily be taken with a
grain of salt. The cumulation of evidence on comparative
plant sizes, read in the context of detailed findings on plant-
scale economies in United States manufacturing industries,
suggests a general tendency in all of the other countries
studied except the United Kingdom toward a very high incidence among industries of at least some significant inefficiencies of small-scale plants affecting production by over
half of the working force employed in manufacturing production, as opposed to 30 per cent or less of the corresponding
working force in the United States. This is perhaps not a
staggering difference, but it is worthy of note. Possible reasons for this difference will be discussed in the concluding
chapter.

9. "Reasonably efficient" plant scales in the U.S. data have been
defined as scales for which unit costs are no more than 3 or 4 per cent
above minimum attainable; thus "inefficient" plants have a unit-cost
disadvantage of 5 per cent or more. The size class intervals within which
reasonably efficient plants fall have been established accordingly, on the
assumption that at least 70 per cent of each industry output is supplied
by reasonably efficient plants in the United States, this assumption resting
on the detailed study of 20 U.S. industries.

4 COMPARATIVE COMPANY CONCENTRATION IN SELECTED MANUFACTURING INDUSTRIES

We now turn to the comparison of the eight countries under study in terms of the "degree of seller concentration," or degree of concentration of control of capacity or output in the hands of relatively few firms, in each of a substantial sample of selected industries.

Seller concentration or "company concentration" within any individual industry is of course generally described by the absolute number and the proportionally measured size distribution of separate and independent firms within the industry. For summary purposes, it is usually measured in any industry by the percentages of the total shipments, output, capacity, or employment of the industry accounted for by various absolute numbers of "largest" firms in the industry. Compilations from the Census of Manufactures of the United States for recent years thus show for each census industry the percentages of value of shipments controlled by the largest four, eight, twenty, and fifty firms in the industry. Similar compilations for the United Kingdom and Canada, each based on a single census, show in a systematic fashion only the percentages of value added or employment controlled by the three largest firms in each industry, whereas a recent compilation based on a Japanese census shows the proportion of value of output in each industry controlled by the largest one, three, five, and ten firms. For the other four countries in our sample no systematic measures of concentration of industry control by firms have been compiled from census data, and we have had to develop our own seller concentration measures for as many industries as possible from a large variety of sources. In these cases, we have generally tried to determine so far as possible at least the proportions of individual industry outputs or capacities controlled by the largest one, three, and eight firms, to facilitate comparisons with countries for which concentration measures based on census data are available.

Given the limitations of data available for all countries except the United States, our attention has necessarily focused on the degree of concentration of control of individual industries in very few firms—in the largest three or four firms mostly, with attention as data permit to control by the single largest firm, the largest eight or ten firms, and occasionally to control by intermediate absolute numbers of firms. That is to say, we have information for the various countries primarily bearing on the degree of "top-level" concentration, referring to a very few largest firms per industry, but lack information on "low-level" concentration as measured by the proportion of industries controlled by larger absolute numbers of largest firms. In consequence our intercountry comparisons of the degree of seller concentration in individual industries are effectively comparisons of the degree of top-level concentration only. We are able to compare countries with respect to the percentages of individual industries controlled by the largest three or four or sometimes eight firms, but not with respect to the percentages of the same industries controlled by the largest twenty, thirty, or fifty firms. Our intercountry comparisons of seller concentration by industries are thus incomplete, since they do not refer to the full concentration profiles of individual industries, and some potentially significant intercountry differences in seller concentration are not revealed.

The data we do have, however, centering on top-level seller concentration, reveal that aspect of the number and size distribution of sellers in any industry which is generally considered most relevant for purposes of economic analysis. This is of course because the degree of top-level seller concentration is generally felt to be closely associated with the degree of monopoly or joint monopoly power possessed by sellers in an industry, and to be the main basis for distinguishing among industries which are respectively single-firm monopolies, highly concentrated oligopolies, moderately concentrated oligopolies, and industries of relatively atomistic structure. The data on seller concentration moreover are generally superior to those on plant concentration discussed in the preceding chapter, both because they refer directly to actual percentages of industries controlled by specific numbers of firms (and are not simply estimates of percentages controlled calculated from frequency distributions of firms grouped by size categories) and because the industries for which they have been calculated are in numerous cases more narrowly defined and correspond more closely to "theoretical" industries for which seller concentration has a definite analytical significance.

The intercountry comparisons of seller or company concentration which we will present involve 42 industries in all, generally corresponding to "four-digit" industries in the classification of the Census of Manufactures of the United States. We have data on all 42 of them, however, only for the United States. In each of the other seven countries, seller concentration data on only part of the total number

TABLE 4–1

List of Forty-two Industries for Which Seller Concentration Is Compared,
in Order of Four-Firm Seller Concentration in the United States

Industries	Percentage of Industry Controlled in U.S. in 1954 by 4 Largest Firms	8 Largest Firms	Number of Countries Covered	Corresponding Plant Concentration Data Available
Primary aluminum	100	—	7	no
Passenger automobiles	98	99	8	no
Electric lamps	93	97	3	yes
Locomotives	91	98	3	no
Flat glass	90	99	2	no
Primary copper	86	n.a.[a]	4	no
Primary lead	n.a.	100	4	no
Soap and glycerine	85	89	3	yes
Typewriters	83	99	3	no
Cigarettes	82	99	5	no
Sulfuric acid	82	95	4	no
Tin cans	80	89	3	no
Tires and tubes	79	91	3	no
Trucks	77	93	6	no
Matches	74	93	7	no
Tractors	73	88	4	no
Explosives	72	92	2	yes
Railway cars	64	81	3	no
Distilled liquors	64	79	3	yes
Steel ingots	64	76	8	yes
Shortening and cooking oils	55	80	3	no
Primary zinc	53	87	4	no
Motorcycles	50	77	5	no
Aircraft	47	76	5	yes
Plastic materials	47	69	3	yes
Shipbuilding and repairing	43	58	7	yes
Flour and meal	40	52	7	yes
Farm machinery (excl. tractors)	38	51	2	no
Petroleum refining	32	55	8	yes
Textile machinery	32	46	4	no
Cement	31	48	8	yes
Pulp mills	29	42	3	yes
Canned and preserved fruits, vegetables	28	39	4	yes
Beer and ale	27	41	5	yes
Paints and varnishes	27	37	3	yes
Pharmaceutical preparations	25	44	4	yes
Hosiery mills	22	31	4	yes
Wool yarn	20	32	5	no
Paper and paperboard	19	31	7	yes
Machine tools	19	29	5	no
Cotton textiles	18	29	5	yes
Sawmills and planing mills	7	11	4	yes

[a] Not available.

Sources: See Tables 4–2 to 4–8, and Appendix Tables A–1 to A–8.

Comparative Company Concentration

of industries are available, either because of general unavailability of data or because of intercountry differences in the
definitions of industries which preclude valid intercountry
comparisons. Thus we have concentration data comparable
to United States data for 32 manufacturing industries in the
United Kingdom, 25 in Japan, 19 in France, 19 in Italy, 22
in Canada, 16 in India, and only 7 in Sweden. The lowest
representations are for countries for which no systematic
census data on seller concentration are available—France,
Italy, India, and Sweden. (A somewhat larger number of
industries could in fact be compared for the United States,
United Kingdom, Canada, and Japan alone.)

The 42 industries compared are listed in Table 4–1, together with their four-firm and eight-firm concentration
ratios (percentages controlled by the four and eight largest
firms) in the United States, an indication of how many countries are covered for each industry, and a notation as to
whether or not plant concentration data for industries
identically or very similarly defined are available. It should
at once be noted that the sample of industries is dispropor-
tionally weighted by industries which have relatively high
seller concentration in the United States. The extent of this
bias, which resulted from limitations on availability of comparable data for other countries, is suggested by the following
comparison of the percentages of *all* United States manufacturing industries in 1954 falling in four different seller
concentration classes and the corresponding percentages of
the 42 industries listed falling in these classes:

Industries with Four-Firm Concentration Ratio of:	Percentage of all U.S. Manufacturing Industries, 1954	Percentage of 42 U.S. Industries Sampled, 1954
75–100	9.2	33.3
50– 75	23.3	21.4
25– 50	36.2	31.0
0– 25	31.3	14.3

71

Although industries with four-firm concentration ratios in the United States between 25 and 75 are represented in the sample more or less in proportion to their importance among all United States manufacturing industries, industries of very high concentration (above 75 per cent control by four firms) are heavily overrepresented in the sample, and industries of low concentration (below 25 per cent control by four firms) are almost equivalently underrepresented, though there is a substantial representation in the sample in each of the four concentration categories. For whatever importance attaches to it, 55 per cent of the industries in the sample lie at or above the arbitrary 50-per-cent-by-four level, and 45 per cent below this line (as compared to 33 and 67 per cent for all manufacturing industries in the United States). And 57 per cent of the sampled industries have eight-firm concentration ratios above 70, and 43 per cent below (the 70-per-cent-by-eight line having been tentatively established as a divider between oligopolies with and without distinct monopolistic pricing tendencies).[1]

In our intercountry comparisons of seller concentration by industries, the overall findings are thus rather strongly influenced by comparative concentration within industries that are, in the United States and generally in the other countries, very highly concentrated; they are somewhat weakly influenced by comparative concentration in relatively unconcentrated industries. This bias, moreover, may be of some moment. There are general indications that in several of the countries, including at least Italy, India, and Japan and probably France, there is a tendency toward "dual economies" incorporating modern, big business sectors along with "traditional" small business or household enterprise sectors, and that whereas in the modern sectors seller concentration by industries tends to equal or exceed that found in the United States, in the traditional sectors seller concentration

1. See Joe S. Bain, "Relation of Profit Rate to Industry Concentration: American Manufacturing, 1936–40," *Quarterly Journal of Economics, 65* (1951), 293–324.

in all probability tends to fall well below that found in the United States. If the latter tendency is indeed present, it tends to be somewhat obscured in our sample of industries, and due allowance for this should be made in interpreting the statistical comparisons which follow.

In presenting intercountry comparisons of seller concentration by industries, a broad cross-sectional comparison of the sort made with respect to plant concentration has been found not to be feasible, largely because it is possible only for about a dozen industries to find the same concentration measure, such as a three-firm or four-firm concentration ratio, for a majority or more of the eight countries. Such a cross-sectional comparison moreover would either be confusingly complicated or would omit essential information provided by concentration ratios referring to various different absolute numbers of firms. It thus appears that a maximum amount of information on comparative seller concentration can be presented in understandable fashion by comparing each of the seven other countries in turn with the United States, for those industries for which comparable data are available for each country. A cumulative comparison among countries other than the United States will develop as we proceed.

This procedure has substantial further advantages. Comparative seller concentration by industries among countries is presumably interesting because of its implications for intercountry differences in the character of intraindustry competition and in the degree of monopoly or joint monopoly power exercised by the larger sellers in any industry. The extent of the monopoly power is evidently related to the degree of seller concentration as this is revealed by our barebone statistics on percentages of industries controlled by given absolute small numbers of firms, where a "firm" is any independent ownership and/or control unit. But it is also influenced by other things, in particular:

1. The extent and character of governmental control of private manufacturing industries.

2. The general importance of cartelization in private industry, and governmental policy toward cartelization.
3. The extent of government participation as a producer and seller in various manufacturing industries.
4. The importance, if any, of "super control" groups which control the operations of different ostensibly independent firms in the same industry or related industries.
5. The importance in various industries of imports that are competitive with the domestic outputs and that may reduce domestic monopoly power.

It is thus appropriate, in interpreting comparative statistics on seller concentration, to comment on these other matters as they effect each country in turn, and to allow for them in any final evaluation. Though we have not been able to delve deeply into any of these matters for the countries under study, some general observations concerning them can be offered which should be of assistance in judging the probable significance of various intercountry differences in seller concentration in individual industries. The procedure of dealing with each country in turn, as compared to the United States, facilitates the process of going a bit beyond the bare statistics of domestic seller concentration in our intercountry comparisons.

Before turning to these comparisons, some mention of the deficiencies in the data employed is in order. First, the share of an industry controlled by any firm is measured in different and not strictly comparable units for different countries— usually by value of shipments in the United States, by value added in manufacture in the United Kingdom, by employment in Canada, and by value of output in other countries. In addition, market share is measured by capacity for a few industries in some or all countries, and by physical units of output in a few cases. The intercountry differences in the firm size variable which are encountered lend a rough-and-ready aspect to some of the intercountry comparisons. Second, the systems of census enumeration employed in the United States, Canada, and the United Kingdom, which underlie the seller concentration ratios found for these countries, especially as they regard the inclusion of minor nonindustry outputs (or workers) of firms in a given industry and the criteria for including the output of any firm in a given industry, are of a rough-and-ready character and lead to only approximately accurate concentration measures. Moreover, such criteria differ somewhat among these countries, with some resultant minor reduction in the degree of comparability of their statistics.[2] For Japan, we have detailed statistical data on seller concentration from census sources, but lack adequate information on the procedures of census enumeration employed. And for the other four countries, we rely mainly on direct special reports concerning individual industries, from private industry, trade paper, and governmental sources, and perforce accept the reports on faith after cross-checking for accuracy wherever possible. In general, therefore, the data presented can at best be expected in most instances to give only good rough indications of intercountry differences in seller concentration by industries, and not measures as precise as the numbers written down might suggest.

In the following sections of this chapter we will treat the individual countries (each compared to the United States) in the general order of ascending average or modal degree of seller concentration in individual industries, thus dealing in turn with the United Kingdom, Japan, France, Italy, Canada, India, and Sweden. Following a brief summary of the findings of these sections, we will offer in Chapter 5 such comments as evidence available supports concerning the relationship of intercountry differences in seller or company concentration to intercountry differences in plant concentration.

2. For details on this matter, see the major sources cited for these countries on succeeding tables in this chapter.

THE UNITED KINGDOM COMPARED TO
THE UNITED STATES

The general pattern of top-level seller concentration among manufacturing industries in the United States is well known, and was summarized above on page 71. The United Kingdom evidences a tendency toward approximately the same or a slightly lesser degree of concentration of control of industries by a few large firms. This conclusion is based on the comparison of top-level seller concentration in 32 industries in two countries, as presented in Table 4–2. Available data on these 32 manufacturing industries in the United Kingdom, each with a definition closely comparable to that of a corresponding industry in the United States, refer primarily to the proportion of the industry value-added contributed by the largest three firms in each industry, as computed by Evely and Little[3] from data gathered in the 1951 Census of Production of the United Kingdom. These three-firm concentration ratios (together with supplementary data for certain industries) are therefore compared with the four-firm concentration ratios for the same industries in the United States as of 1954, these referring to the proportion of industry shipments accounted for by the largest four firms in each industry.[4]

---

3. Richard Evely and I. M. D. Little, *Concentration in British Industry* (Cambridge, Eng., 1960).

4. In comparing three-firm concentration in one country (here the United Kingdom) with four-firm concentration in another (the United States throughout) for a given industry—with the general purpose of deciding in which country top-level seller concentration is probably higher—no difficulty in making an ordinal ranking is encountered in those cases where the three-firm ratio is approximately equal to or greater than the four-firm ratio, or in those cases where the value of the three-firm ratio is less than 75 per cent of the four-firm ratio. Where the three-firm ratio is appreciably below the four-firm ratio but below it by appreciably less than 25 per cent of the four-firm ratio, however, some

Comparative Company Concentration

A survey of Table 4–2 reveals that for the 32 industries, top-level seller concentration was about the same or slightly less or greater in the United Kingdom in 9 cases, was significantly lower in 12 cases, and significantly higher in 11 cases. The general concentration picture in the two countries is thus roughly the same, but if there is a difference it is reflected in some slight mean tendency for manufacturing industries in the United Kingdom to have lower seller concentration, particularly because the intercountry discrepancy in concentration is on the average greater for industries in which the United Kingdom is less concentrated than for those in which it is more concentrated. The identities of the very highly concentrated industries (with four-firm concentration ratios above 70) are the same in 6 cases in the two countries, but there are 4 industries which are very highly concentrated in the United States but not in the United Kingdom, and 4 which are highly concentrated in the United Kingdom but not in the United States. The United Kingdom tends toward significantly lower concentration than the

---

rough "conversion factor" must be employed mentally in guessing approximately what three-firm ratio is linked with a given four-firm ratio, or what four-firm ratio is linked with a given three-firm ratio, as a basis for comparing top-level seller concentration as between the pair of countries for the industry in question. No single conversion factor of course will be approximately correct for all industries, because of a distinct lack of uniformity of the size distribution of the largest four firms as among industries. On the basis of as many full size distributions as we have been able to observe, however, we have arrived at an approximate average conversion factor for all-purpose use in cases where detailed size-distribution data are unavailable. This conversion factor is based on the assumption that on the average the fourth largest firm in an industry controls about one-sixth of the combined market share of the four largest firms. In this case, the estimated three-firm ratio for an industry is five-sixths of the known four-firm ratio, and the estimated four-firm ratio is six-fifths of the known three-firm ratio. Individual conversion ratios as low as one-tenth or as high as one-fifth, however, might turn out to be appropriate in individual cases.

TABLE 4–2

United Kingdom and United States—Comparative Percentages of
Thirty-two Industries Controlled by the Largest Firms,
1951 and 1954

PERCENTAGES OF SHIPMENTS OR VALUE ADDED

	United States 1954	United Kingdom 1951			
	Value of Shipments	Value Added by Largest Firms			
Industries[a]	Four Largest Firms	Three Largest	Four Largest	Five Largest	Six Largest
Primary aluminum[b]	100	43	—	—	—
Passenger automobiles[c]	98	74	—	—	—
Electric lamps	93	56	—	—	—
Locomotives	91	53	—	—	—
Flat glass	90	51	—	—	—
Cigarettes[d]	82	74	—	—	—
Tires and tubes	79	73	—	—	—
Trucks[c]	77	86	—	—	—
Matches	74	—	—	—	86
Explosives	72	—	—	—	91
Steel ingots	64	32	—	—	—
Railway cars	64	25	—	—	—
Distilled liquors	64	—	—	—	73
Shortening and cooking oils	55	79	—	—	—
Primary zinc	53	—	—	82	—
Motorcycles	50	87	—	—	—
Aircraft	47	47	—	—	—
Plastic materials	47	51	—	—	—
Shipbuilding and repairing	43	23	—	—	—
Flour and meal	40	46	—	—	—
Farm machinery (excl. tractors)	38	40	—	—	—
Textile machinery	32	36	—	—	—
Petroleum refining[e]	32	93	—	—	—
Cement	31	—	89	—	—
Canned and preserved fruits, vegetables	28	21	—	—	—
Beer and ale	27	11	—	—	—
Paints and varnishes	27	20	—	—	—
Pharmaceutical products	25	24	—	—	—
Hosiery mills	22	12	—	—	—
Wool yarn	20	12	—	—	—
Cotton textiles	18	4	—	—	—
Sawmills and planing mills	7	5	—	—	—

[a]Industry classifications for U.S. are census four-digit industries; for U.K. they are similar unless otherwise noted.
[b]Includes magnesium and alloys for U.K.
[c]Data refer to 1959; market shares in units of output.
[d]Includes all tobacco products for U.K.
[e]Data refer to 1959; market shares in throughput capacity.

Sources: U.S. Senate, Committee on the Judiciary, Subcommittee on Antitrust and Monopoly, *Concentration in American Industry,* 85th Cong., 1st Sess. (Washington, D.C., G.P.O., 1957); Richard Evely and I. M. D. Little, *Concentration in British Industry* (Cambridge, Eng., 1960); Iron and Steel Board, *Development in the Iron and Steel Industry: A Special Report, 1957* (London, 1958); *Oil and Gas Journal* (Mar. 31 and Dec. 28, 1959); Duncan Burn, ed., *The Structure of British Industries* (London, 1959); A. G. Donnithorne, *British Rubber Manufacturing, An Economic Study of Innovation* (London, 1958); private industry sources, for data on the passenger automobile and truck industries.

United States mostly in industries which in the United States are either very highly concentrated or quite unconcentrated. It tends toward significantly higher concentration mainly in industries which in the United States are in the middle ranges of concentration.

One aspect of intercountry differences in concentration not revealed by the ratios in Table 4–2 concerns the extent of the dominance of single firms in individual industries. There are no cases of single-firm dominance in the industries listed for the United States. In the United Kingdom, well over half the output of the match industry is supplied by one firm, and two-thirds of the output of the cement industry by one firm.[5] In the rubber tire industry, one firm (Dunlop) makes about 47 per cent of all tire sales and about 72 per cent of the sales of original equipment tires for passenger automobiles.[6] Any slight tendency toward lower seller concentration in British manufacturing industries as measured by three-firm concentration ratios is thus in part counterbalanced by some incidence of partial monopolies, not found in the United States.

In the manufacturing sector, there is of course in the United States practically no direct control of or interference with private enterprise. Cartels are illegal per se, and restraints of trade, monopolization, and mergers which tend

5. Duncan Burn, ed., *Structure of British Industries,* National Institute of Economic and Social Research, *1* (London, 1959).

6. A. G. Donnithorne, *British Rubber Manufacturing* (London, 1958), p. 47.

substantially to lessen competition are systematically attacked under the antitrust laws. In the United Kingdom there is also very little direct governmental interference in the manufacturing sector, except in the iron and steel industry. There, after nationalization and subsequent denationalization of the industry, an Iron and Steel Board exercises general supervision over the industry, and is empowered to fix maximum prices and to examine and at its discretion veto the investment programs of steel companies (although this veto power has been sparingly used). As to manufacturing industries generally, formal cartels are not recognized, and under the Restrictive Practices Act of 1956 the government is empowered to investigate and if necessary eliminate restrictive practices in industry and trade, the main emphasis falling on the elimination of collusive agreements. It is probably fair to say that the British "antitrust" policy is comparatively softer and less vigorously pursued than that of the United States and that enforcement measures are comparatively toothless. The comparative strength of collusion in restraint of trade in the United States and the United Kingdom in the years since World War II has never really been assessed, but the climate seems to be more favorable to effective collusion in the United Kingdom. But both countries have substantially free-enterprise systems in the manufacturing sector, and neither system is greatly influenced by real cartelization.

There is effectively no participation by the government as a producer in manufacturing industries in the United Kingdom, as is also the case in the United States. And though powerful financial concerns and large holdings by wealthy families are found in both countries, there is a substantial lack of evidence of the importance of real "super-control" groups, such as might actually control and coordinate the operations of groups of ostensibly independent private firms.

A final matter concerns the possible dilution of the monopoly power inherent in domestic seller concentration in various industries by imports of competitive supplies. Imports are of minor importance in this regard in all the industries in the United States which are here compared with British industries, and generally of little importance also in the United Kingdom in the same industries. The principal exceptions identified from incomplete data involve primary zinc, where United Kingdom domestic production is only about one-third of production plus imports, and in petroleum refining, where imports account for about one-fourth of the national supply of refined petroleum products. In the latter instance in particular however the imports are possibly or probably controlled by the principal domestic firms, so that effective seller concentration is not reduced. Concentration data for the United Kingdom for the primary copper and primary lead industries are not available, but for both of these products the United Kingdom is predominantly dependent on imports. The potential competition-increasing effects of imports in British domestic markets for manufactured goods deserve a much more searching examination than we have been able to give them in connection with this study.

JAPAN COMPARED TO THE UNITED STATES

A comparison of seller concentration in Japanese industries with concentration in counterpart industries in the United States could at present better be presented through a motion picture, which we do not have, than through a still photograph taken at a moment in time, which we do have. This is because following the dissolution of the zaibatsu (vertically integrated and diversified family holding company systems) and the institution of antitrust laws under the American occupation after 1945—programs which had appreciable effects on the structure of individual industries as well as on the economic power structure of Japan—the period since 1954 has seen a reconsolidation of the zaibatsu

TABLE 4–3

Japan and United States—Comparative Percentages of Twenty-five
Industries Controlled by the Largest Firms, 1958 and 1954

	PERCENTAGES OF SHIPMENTS OR VALUE OF OUTPUT CONTROLLED				
	United States 1954		Japan 1958		
	Value of Shipments by Largest Firms		Value of Output by Largest Firms		
Industries[a]	Four Largest	Eight Largest	Single Largest	Three Largest	Ten Largest
Primary aluminum	100	—	49	100	—
Primary lead	n.a.	100	32	77	100[b]
Passenger automobiles[c]	98	99	34	76	100
Electric lamps	93	97	37	64	79
Flat glass	90	99	58	100	—
Primary copper	86	n.a.	23	60	77
Soap	85	89	n.a.	32	42[d]
Sulfuric acid	82	95	9	25	58
Tin cans	80	89	52	79	96
Trucks[c]	77	93	33	57	93
Matches	74	93	19	n.a.	46
Steel ingots	64	76	23	52	80
Primary zinc	53	87	32	77	100[b]
Motorcycles	50	77	31	55	85
Shipbuilding and repairing	43	58	15	31	67
Flour and meal	40	52	28	53	66
Petroleum refining[e]	32	55	16	41	84
Cement	31	48	17	48	82
Pulp mills	29	42	13	27	59
Beer and ale	27	41	39	98	100[b]
Pharmaceutical products	25	44	23	55	95
Wool yarn	20	32	6	10	18
Paper and paperboard	19	31	19	30	64
Machine tools	19	29	8	25	58
Cotton textiles	18	29	3	7	18

[a]Industry classifications for U.S. are census four-digit industries; for Japan they are similar unless otherwise noted.
[b]100 per cent controlled by five firms.
[c]Data refer to 1959; market shares in units of output.
[d]Japanese data refer to 1953.
[e]Data refer to 1959; market shares in throughput capacity.

Sources: U.S. Senate, *Concentration in American Industry;* tables prepared by the Japanese Fair Trade Commission (unpublished); *Oil and Gas Journal* (Mar. 31 and Dec. 28, 1959); private industry sources, for data on passenger automobile and truck industries.

in somewhat altered form, the partial emasculation of the new antitrust policy, and a process of reorganization of the control of Japanese industries which is evidently still under way. Whereas seller concentration in manufacturing industries in the United States has generally tended to remain relatively stable at least since 1935, similar seller concentration in Japan is still evolving in a process of reaction to the severe displacements wrought during the occupation, and probably has not achieved a steady state as yet.

With these cautionary remarks, we turn to a comparison of seller concentration in Japan and the United States for 25 comparably defined manufacturing industries, in Table 4–3. The table draws on Japanese data which were prepared by the Japanese Fair Trade Commission, made available in unpublished form, and then translated from Japanese to English. The data refer generally to 1958 and measure control in terms of value of output;[7] these are compared with 1954 data for the United States, which measure control in terms of value of shipments. In the Japanese data, ostensibly independent firms which may fall under the control or influence of a reconstituted zaibatsu are considered to be separate units and are not combined. Such revisions in the Japanese seller concentration data as would result from combining the market shares of such firms will be discussed below.[8]

On the average for the industries represented, top-level seller concentration is about the same or slightly greater in Japan than it is in the United States. Japanese industries are significantly more concentrated in 11 of 25 cases, significantly

7. Unfortunately, we could not avail ourselves of two official studies published by the Fair Trade Commission in 1956 and 1958, entitled (titles translated to English): *Recent Trends in the Concentration of Production in Major Industries* (1956), and *Concentration of Production in Major Industries* (1958).

8. 1958 data for the United States are now available, but industry concentration ratios shown by them do not differ enough from 1954 ratios to affect our comparisons at all significantly.

less concentrated in 9 cases, and have about the same or slightly higher or lower concentration in 5 cases. Five of the industries are very highly concentrated in both countries, whereas 4 industries which are highly concentrated in the United States are not in Japan, and 4 industries which are highly concentrated in Japan are not in the United States. Japan tends toward significantly less concentration in industries which are highly concentrated in the United States, and toward significantly greater concentration in industries which in the United States have relatively low concentration ratios. This comparison however may easily give a false impression concerning comparative concentration in all Japanese industries, since there is in the sample presented no more than a token representation of important Japanese industries in the food, clothing, wood products, and cottage-industry sectors, which are in general unquestionably much less concentrated than counterpart industries in the United States. It is primarily in the "modern" and "heavy" industries that seller concentration in Japan is roughly on a par with that in the United States.

Dominant control of manufacturing industries in Japan by single firms, as shown by Table 4–3, is generally not found, and oligopolistic market structures featuring a "big three" or "big four" of firms, like those found in the United States, are common in the concentrated industries. This situation is in some part attributable to deconcentration fostered under the occupation, but much more strongly explicable by the policies of the prewar zaibatsu, which, like their postoccupation successors, generally featured a diversification of investment among numerous industries in lieu of a concentrated investment in a few which would have given them dominant or quasi-monopoly positions in individual industries. The major exceptions to the rule involve single-firm government monopolies in salt, camphor, tobacco products, and alcohol.

In referring to governmental interference with or control

of private industry, we will confine ourselves to the contemporary situation. After contributing a very high percentage of total investment during the reconstruction period after World War II (channeled in large part through the zaibatsu banks), the Japanese government followed the policy of influencing business decisions in such a way as to control or direct the pattern of economic development through selective measures of tax relief, favorable credit terms and other financial assistance, and export promotion, shifting the emphasis in development among industries and sectors. In recent years it has been encouraging development in steel and shipbuilding, for example, and endeavoring to check further growth in textiles and fertilizers.[9] This sort of governmental intervention implements national planning, but does not per se significantly encourage or discourage competition in the private sector, where ownership and control of nearly all productive activity is vested.

As regards policies toward competition, the strong Anti-Monopoly Law of 1947, which aimed at dissolving the zaibatsu and preventing their revival, deconcentration, control of new combinations, and the prohibition of collusion generally, has been emasculated by amendment. The law now permits cartels when necessary to deal with depression or to rationalize industry (the prime asserted justification of cartels the world over); permits firms to hold stocks in competing companies if competition is not substantially restrained thereby; legalizes resale price maintenance in certain lines; eases restrictions on mergers; and increases the percentage (from 5 to 10 per cent) of stock that a bank is permitted to hold in any nonfinancial company.[10] In addition, special legislation has provided for voluntary and compulsory cartelization of small-business industries and concerns in

9. Economic Planning Agency, *New Long-Range Economic Plan of Japan 1961–1970, Doubling National Income Plan* (Tokyo, 1961).

10. U.S. Department of Commerce, Bureau of Foreign Commerce, *Investment in Japan* (Washington, D.C., G.P.O., 1956), pp. 82–83.

foreign trade. Although Japan still ostensibly has an anti-trust policy, it is looking increasingly like a pro-cartel policy with minimal controls on monopolization and restraint of trade.[11] It is also a policy of reliance on concentrated and, to a considerable extent, cartelized private industry, as the government does not participate in manufacturing except in the case of the few state monopolies mentioned above.

This postreconstruction trend is consistent with the re-emergence of the zaibatsu. In its pre-World War II form, the zaibatsu was typically a financial, commercial, and industrial empire held by a wealthy family or related families, its con-stituent parts being more or less fully and formally controlled through a top holding company, its major operating sub-sidiaries, and a frequently intricate network of lesser sub-sidiary or affiliated corporations. It typically included a bank, a trading company, and operating corporations in each of a number of manufacturing and mining industries (occasion-ally more than one in a single industry), most but not all of which stood in a loosely vertical relationship to each other, so that a type of interindustry vertical integration was ac-complished by the zaibatsu. We will not pause here to review the prewar position of the various zaibatsu in Japan, the history of their dissolution under the postwar American occupation and of their subsequent reemergence in somewhat altered form, or the details of which ones survived to re-emerge and how much of its size and strength each had lost as the result of the dissolution episode. All of these matters

11. Ibid., p. 83. Cartels for smaller firms are permitted by the Smaller Enterprise Stabilization Act of 1952 and for foreign trade in the Export-Import Trading Law of 1952. The Ministry of International Trade and Industry has initiated cartels on its own accord. A recent tabulation of cartel strength in Japan reports 5 depression cartels, 4 nationalization cartels, 150 export-import cartels, 57 small-enterprise cartels, and 34 Ministry cartels. See Eugene Rotwein, "Economic Concentration and Monopoly in Japan," *Journal of Political Economy, 122* (1964), p. 273.

have been covered in great detail in a sufficiency of books.[12]

Suffice it to say, the zaibatsu in Japan began reconsolidating and formally reasserting themselves after 1954, although in altered form. The old zaibatsu names were reassumed by banks and the former subsidiaries of the prewar zaibatsu holding companies and the great zaibatsu trading companies were rehabilitated. The postreconstruction zaibatsu however apparently takes the form of an alliance of ostensibly independent firms which are linked together through common affiliation with a single bank, through legally limited holdings by the bank of their stock shares, and through a maze of interlocking stockholdings and interlocking directorates—rather than that of a corporate system controlled by a top holding company. A "group affiliate financing system," adopted by the large banks held by the prewar zaibatsu, was a principal instrument in bringing together these new coalitions. As the *Oriental Economist* puts it: "In very general terms, the present zaibatsu groups are held together mainly by intra-group cross-holdings of corporate stock, which are supplemented by normal business transactions within the group, including the trading company, and by the financing afforded by the group banking institutions."[13]

The extent to which or the sense in which the postoccupation zaibatsu is really a "super-control" group as opposed to

12. See, e.g., G. C. Allen, *Japan's Economic Recovery* (New York and London, 1960); T. A. Bisson, *Zaibatsu Dissolution in Japan* (Berkeley, Calif., 1954); J. B. Cohen, *Japan's Postwar Economy* (Bloomington, Ind., 1954); W. W. Lockwood, *The Economic Development of Japan* (Princeton, N.J., 1954); Eleanor Hadley, "Trust Busting in Japan," *Harvard Business Review* (July, 1948), pp. 425–40. See also *Oriental Economist*, Feb.–June, 1961, "Zaibatsu Leadership Race" (in five parts); Rotwein; and Kozo Yamamura, "Zaibatsu, Pre-War and Zaibatsu, Postwar," *Journal of Asian Studies, 23* (1964), 539–54.

13. *Oriental Economist*, "Zaibatsu Leadership Race," Part I (February, 1961), pp. 74–75.

a sort of strong alliance of independent companies is debatable,[14] but whether or not there is a true and effective centralization of control in any zaibatsu, it is clear that the member firms of each one engage heavily in reciprocal dealing inter se, so that the membership as a whole functions somewhat after the fashion of units in a vertically integrated enterprise, with a flow within the zaibatsu groups of raw materials to basic products to more finished products to trading and shipping. This pattern is consistent with the fact that the postoccupation zaibatsu group, like the prewar zaibatsu, is diversified among numerous industries which stand in roughly vertical or complementary relationships in the total process of production and distribution.

The three dominant surviving or reconstituted zaibatsu are Mitsubishi (the largest), and Mitsui and Sumitomo (each about three-fifths as large as Mitsubishi). Together they "control" about 40 per cent of Japan's "big business," even excluding important loosely affiliated concerns. Each, in addition to diversified engagement in manufacturing industries, is importantly engaged in mining, transportation, trading, real estate, banking, casualty insurance, and electric and gas utilities. As to manufacturing, firms in the Mitsubishi group are engaged in petroleum refining, primary copper and zinc, machine tools, industrial electrical equipment, television sets, major household electrical appliances, shipbuilding, automobiles, industrial chemicals, rayon, glass, cement, ceramics, and textiles. Firms in the Mitsui group are engaged in primary copper and zinc, shipbuilding, industrial chemicals, rayon, chemical fibers, machinery, textiles, and food processing. Sumitomo firms produce in the copper, aluminum, steel, electric wire and cable, industrial chemical, glass, machinery, ceramics, and textile industries.

Firms associated with the principal zaibatsu, individually and collectively, are thus major participants in a broad band

14. See Yamamura for a discussion of the position refuting the notion of zaibatsu revival.

of Japanese manufacturing industries, but they are not significantly present in all of them. Moreover, it is unusual for a single zaibatsu to be represented in an individual industry by more than one firm, and typically a zaibatsu firm is not the largest firm in any industry, but simply among the largest. Firms associated with zaibatsu are generally the second, third, or fourth most important firms in oligopolistic industries.

There are some exceptions to the second rule, as in many industrial chemicals and in shipbuilding, where the firm or firms associated with a single zaibatsu is the largest firm, and a few to the first rule, where two or more firms associated with a single zaibatsu operate in the same industry, though the incidence of the latter phenomenon has in recent years been reduced by mergers. In any event, recognizing the two or more firms in an industry associated with a single zaibatsu as a single firm (and this is less than axiomatic) does not much change the degree of seller concentration in individual industries. A thorough check of multiple representation of individual zaibatsu in individual industries has revealed only the following changes in seller concentration in individual industries resulting from the recognition of two or more firms associated with the same zaibatsu being considered a single firm:[15]

FIVE-FIRM CONCENTRATION RATIOS

Industries	Not recognizing zaibatsu affiliations	Recognizing zaibatsu affiliations
Steel ships	45.1	56.1
Passenger-car chassis	92.6	97.9
Foreign-style paper	48.0	55.1
Sulfuric acid	38.4	42.5
Rayon filament	82.1	82.4
Vinyl chloride	54.3	59.6
Ammonium sulfate	54.9	63.4
Urea	72.7	79.7

15. *Oriental Economist* (February, 1961), pp. 74–75.

The effects on horizontal intraindustry seller concentration of zaibatsu controls of numerous firms are thus scattered and generally slight. It seems very likely however that the large volume of vertical supplier-customer transactions and reciprocal trading within each individual zaibatsu substantially reduces the scope and effectiveness of horizontal competition within many Japanese industries, so that more monopoly power is associated with given degrees of intra-industry seller concentration than would otherwise be the case. When this consideration is taken into account, together with present governmental policies favoring cartels, we must conclude that although roughly comparable in terms of bare-bone seller concentration ratios, Japanese industry has at present an appreciably more monopolistic structure than American or British industry, at least so far as "modern" and "heavy" industries are concerned.

A final matter to be considered is the importance of imports as a source of competition with Japanese domestic manufacturers. These generally do not seem to be important except in the case of primary lead, where imports supply about 30 per cent of the market, and of paper, where imports supply about 40 per cent. In both of these industries, the domestic seller concentration data for Japan give a somewhat exaggerated impression of probable monopoly power.[16]

FRANCE COMPARED TO THE UNITED STATES

Top-level seller concentration in French manufacturing industries tends to be substantially higher than that in comparable industries in the United States, the United Kingdom, and Japan. This finding is suggested by Table 4–4,

16. Rotwein (above, n. 11) calculated the ratio of imports to domestic production for 90 Japanese manufacturing industries and found that in over half of these imports would reduce seller concentration by 2 per cent or less; in 23 they would reduce concentration by 5 per cent or less, and in 7 would reduce concentration by more than 5 per cent.

which compares seller concentration in the United States and in France in 19 industries of comparable definition. The United States data refer to 1954 and value of shipments and are based on the 1954 Census of Manufactures. The French data refer generally to 1959 or 1960 sales or value of output; they are not based on a census, and as suggested by the listing of sources on Table 4–4 have been developed from a variety of official and unofficial sources. A rather heavy reliance has been placed on data listed in "Les 500 Premières Sociétés Françaises,"[17] wherein data on the sales of principal firms were obtained which could be compared with official data on the total volume of sales in various French industries. We do not regard these data as either highly accurate or grossly inaccurate.

Of the 19 French industries, 11 are significantly more concentrated than their counterparts in the United States, 4 are significantly less concentrated, and 4 have about the same or slightly higher or lower seller concentration. Seven industries are very highly concentrated in both countries, and two additional industries are very highly concentrated in France. It is noteworthy that French industries are substantially more concentrated than counterpart American industries in four cases in which American industries are themselves very highly concentrated—the aluminum, sulfuric acid, cigarette, and match industries (in the latter two cases because the industries in France are state monopolies). French industries have significantly lower concentration than counterpart American industries entirely in industries which in the United States have moderate to low concentration. The segment of industries for which this is true is unquestionably underrepresented in the sample of industries presented in Table 4–4. If it were more fully represented, we would find a substantial fraction of French industries with lower concentration than found in the United States, as is

17. *Entreprise,* no. 316, Sept. 23, 1961.

TABLE 4-4

France and United States—Comparative Percentages of Nineteen Industries Controlled by the Largest Firms, 1959–60 and 1954

PERCENTAGES OF SHIPMENTS OR SALES CONTROLLED

Industries[a]	United States 1954 Value of Shipments by Largest Firms		France 1959–60 Sales or Output in Largest Firms				
	Four Largest	Eight Largest	Single Largest	Two Largest	Three Largest	Five Largest	Eight Largest
Primary aluminum	100	—	81	100[b]	—	—	—
Passenger automobiles[c]	98	99	39	—	79	—	100[d]
Cigarettes	82	99	100	—	—	—	—
Sulfuric acid	82	95	60	—	—	—	n.a.[e]
Tires and tubes	79	91	28	—	67	75[f]	—
Trucks[e]	77	93	32	—	78	—	100
Matches	74	93	100	—	—	—	—
Tractors	73	88	38	—	76	—	100
Steel ingots	64	77	16	—	40	—	83
Motorcycles	50	77	35	—	74	—	85

Aircraft	47	76	38	—	62	—	69
Shipbuilding and repairing	43	58	25	—	57	—	90
Flour and meal	40	52	n.a.	—	12	—	19
Petroleum refining[g]	32	55	35	—	72	—	100
Cement	31	48	23	—	52	—	73
Canned and preserved fruits, vegetables	28	39	9	—	—	14	n.a.
Beer and ale	27	41	17	—	—	25	32
Hosiery mills	22	31	2	—	5	—	n.a.
Paper and paperboard	19	31	n.a.	—	14	—	27

[a] Industry classifications for U.S. are census four-digit industries; for France they are similar unless otherwise noted.

[b] French percentages refer to industry capacity.

[c] Data refer to 1959; market shares in units of output.

[d] 100 per cent controlled by seven firms.

[e] Not available.

[f] French percentages refer to 1955.

[g] Data refer to 1959; market shares in throughput capacity.

Sources: U.S. Senate, *Concentration in American Industry;* Institut National de la Statistique et des Études Économiques, *Annuaire statistique de la France, 1961,* 67 (Paris, 1962); Ministère des Finances, *Statistiques et Études Financières,* No. 147 (March, 1961); "Les 500 Premières Sociétés françaises," *Entreprise,* No. 316 (Sept. 23, 1961); U.S. Department of State, Foreign Service Despatch No. 9, *French Aluminum Industry—1960* (July, 1961); *Oil and Gas Journal* (Mar. 31 and Dec. 28, 1959); *La Vie française* (March 2 and 16, 1962).

true also of Japan, though extremely unconcentrated cottage industry is by no means as important in France as it is in Japan.

As compared with the United States, the United Kingdom, and Japan, France has a greater incidence of extremely high seller concentration by industries than do these other countries. This tendency is reflected in part in the single-firm domination of an industry in three cases—in cigarettes and matches, which are government monopolies, and in aluminum, where a single firm controls 81 per cent of all sales and two firms account for all sales.

There is a considerable degree of governmental control of private industry in France. General economic planning (under Plans 1, 2, 3, and 4 to date) establishes production targets and investment requirements for priority sectors of industry. The General Planning Commission employs "power through persuasion" and through consultation, using a number of individual planning commissions. A great emphasis has been placed on the reorganization of the French steel industry, still privately owned, and substantial changes in it, involving increased concentration and lessened competition, have been wrought. Further, the government has endeavored to overcome the tendency in some other basic industries toward dispersion of production among many small firms by encouraging mergers.

Credit rationing was used to direct investment during the postwar inflationary period. Selective price controls were retained for some time in the postwar period, but have generally been abandoned or become nominal since 1960.[18]

Industry cartelization is relatively common, as is suggested by the administration of the "modern" antitrust legislation adopted in 1953. This law established a commission to investigate price agreements in industry, but was not directed

18. John Sheahan, *Promotion and Control of Industry in Postwar France* (Cambridge, Mass., 1963); John and Anne-Marie Hackett, *Economic Planning in France* (London, 1963).

at mergers. The commission in its policy distinguishes between "good" and "bad" cartels, but details on its criteria for awarding gold stars and black marks to cartels are not available. In general it would be fair to say that France operates with recognized cartelization and under a policy which encourages increasing seller concentration and does not attempt to reduce existing concentration. The development of the Common Market may ultimately reduce the significance of high seller concentration in French industries, but results are slow in coming.

The French manufacturing sector differs from those of the countries previously discussed in that the government has fully nationalized a few industries and operates a firm in competition with private firms in at least two others. Public utilities and coal mining are fully nationalized; cigarettes and matches are government monopolies. In addition, one government firm operates in the petroleum refining industry along with private firms, and the government owns and operates the largest motor vehicle firm, Renault, which accounts for about 39 per cent of passenger-car production and 32 per cent of truck production in France. The effect of these government operations in competition with private firms on the character and intensity of competition and the resultant market performance is difficult to appraise, although it does not appear that government competition is of a yardstick sort aimed at securing more competitive performance. It is true however that in the motor vehicle industry Renault has assumed the role of a leader in investment, general sales promotion, promotion of export sales, and product innovation.

It is hard to identify in France any "super-control" groups with organization and cohesion comparable to that found in the postoccupation Japanese zaibatsu. There has been considerable talk about such groups existing in France, but they would seem to represent mainly either general "influence groups" built around financial institutions plus a few very wealthy families with widespread industrial holdings—a fairly common phenomenon in any of the countries being studied.

Import competition is not significant in the domestic markets of most French industries, the emergent Common Market to the contrary notwithstanding, but about 57 per cent of aircraft purchased in France are imported, 35 per cent of machine tools, and 40 per cent of wood pulp. These imports are not such as to modify appreciably the general seller concentration picture previously drawn.

ITALY COMPARED TO THE UNITED STATES

In Italy, top-level seller concentration in the manufacturing industries sampled tends to run appreciably higher than in France and quite substantially higher than in the United States and the United Kingdom. Table 4–5 compares concentration in Italy and the United States in 19 comparable industries. The United States data are those employed in earlier intercountry comparisons; the Italian data, lacking any census-based study, have been assembled from a very wide variety of private and public sources, as suggested by the list of sources in Table 4–5. They refer generally to 1959 or 1960 and to output as a measure of size of firm.

Of the 19 Italian industries, 14 are significantly more concentrated than counterpart industries in the United States, 4 are slightly more or less concentrated or have about the same concentration, and only one (flour) is significantly less concentrated. The incidence of very high three- or four-firm concentration in Italy is not fully revealed by our data, which are reasonably complete only with respect to the proportions of industry outputs controlled by largest single firms, but there are numerous cases in which the largest single firm in an Italian industry controls nearly as great, as great, or greater a proportion of the industry than the four largest

96

TABLE 4–5

Italy and United States—Comparative Percentages of Nineteen
Industries Controlled by the Largest Firms, 1959–60 and 1954

PERCENTAGES OF SHIPMENTS
OR OUTPUT CONTROLLED

Industries[a]	United States 1954 Value of Shipments by Largest Firms		Italy 1959–60 Output by Largest Firms			
	Four Largest	Eight Largest	Single Largest	Two Largest	Three Largest	Eight Largest
Primary aluminum	100	—	61	—	100	—
Passenger automobiles[b]	98	99	84	—	96	100
Primary lead	n.a.[c]	100	28	—	—	n.a.
Typewriters	83	99	60	—	—	n.a.
Sulfuric acid	82	95	81	—	—	n.a.
Trucks[b]	77	93	59	—	92	100
Matches	74	93	70	—	—	n.a.
Tractors	73	88	60	—	—	n.a.
Steel ingots	64	76	38	—	47	72[d]
Primary zinc	53	87	25	—	—	n.a.
Motorcycles	50	77	—	33	—	n.a.
Aircraft	47	76	22	—	—	n.a.
Plastic materials	47	69	43	—	—	n.a.
Shipbuilding and repairing	43	58	67	—	—	n.a.
Flour and meal	40	52	—	4	—	5
Petroleum refining[e]	32	55	14	—	40	66
Cement	31	48	35	46	—	n.a.
Wool yarn	20	32	55	65	—	n.a.
Paper and paperboard	19	31	17	19	—	n.a.

[a]Industry classifications for U.S. census four-digit industries; for Italy
they are similar unless otherwise noted.
[b]Data refer to 1959; market shares in units of output.
[c]Not available.
[d]Data refer to 1956.
[e]Data refer to 1959; market shares in throughput capacity.

Sources: U.S. Senate, Concentration in American Industry; "Italy's 200
Largest Companies," Economic News From Italy (March 23, 1962); summary reports on companies by Banco Commerciale Italiana; annual
company reports of I.R.I. (1960), E.N.I. (1961), Fiat (1960), Olivetti (1961),
Montecatini (1960), Snia Viscosa (1960); U.S. Department of State Foreign

Service despatches on steel, nonferrous metal, motor vehicles, chemicals, paper, and textiles industries; Italian Ministry of Agriculture, special tabulation on flour milling capacity by firms; Organizzazione Apis, *Guida indiriz dell'agricultura italiano* (3d ed. Milan, 1960), on tractors; *Oil and Gas Journal* (March 31 and Dec. 28, 1959); Louis Lister, *Europe's Coal and Steel Community* (New York, 1960); Confederazione generale dell' industria italiana, *Annuario, 1961* (Rome, 1961); Instituto Centrali di Statistica, *Annuario statistico italiano, 1962* (Rome, 1963); Banco di Roma, *Review of Economic Conditions in Italy* (quarterly); private industry sources for data on passenger automobile and truck industries.

firms control in the counterpart industry in the United States. (This is true of passenger automobiles, sulfuric acid, plastics, matches, shipbuilding, cement, paper and paperboard, and wool yarn—in 8 out of 19 cases). In addition, the largest two or three firms in Italian industry apparently rather often match the market share of the largest eight firms in the counterpart American industry, so that there is a tendency in Italy toward tighter-knit oligopolies and partial monopolies.

The sample in Table 4–5, of course gives only token representation to the unconcentrated sphere of Italian manufacturing industry, which has been referred to as having a "dual structure."[19] The same general qualifications thus apply to these findings as were attached to those for France and Japan.

The scope of governmental interference with private industry in Italy is not great. Maximum prices for some basic industrial products are controlled by the Central Price Commission. Cartelization is rather widespread in Italian industry, particularly in the chemical, steel, textile, foodstuff, cellulose, paper, glass, metallurgical product, and "engineering" industries ("engineering" in the Italian lexicon

19. Vera Lutz, *Italy, A Study in Economic Development* (London, 1962). The distinction is drawn between (1) the "technologically efficient," "modern" sphere of Italian industry, concentrated in northern Italy, and (2) the "traditional" industry sector, marked by small, inefficient plants and low wages, and typical of southern Italy. The latter sector is barely represented in our sample of industries, because of lack of Italian data.

covers about all machinery or equipment made out of metal) —a roster which includes the bulk of industries. The postwar policy of the Italian government is to "control" rather than prohibit cartels, and it is not evident that this "control" is of an antimonopoly character.[20]

The Italian government however does exercise a strong influence on the Italian manufacturing sector through direct participation as a producer in numerous industries. Its main instrumentalities are the Instituto per la Ricostruzione (I.R.I.) and the Ente Nazionale Idrocarburi (E.N.I.). I.R.I. is a kind of "Reconstruction Finance Corporation" of the sort we had in the United States, and survived as a governmental holding company controlling subsidiaries in numerous industries which were firms it had assisted financially. It operates in manufacturing and related areas (and in other sectors as well) mainly through six financial subholding companies: Finsider, Finmeccanica, Fincantieri, Finmare, Stet, and Finelettrica; it also controls banks and credit institutions. The general spheres of activity of the six subholding companies are respectively steel, "engineering," shipbuilding, shipping, telephones, and electricity. E.N.I. is a government-owned holding company with many subsidiaries operating in several industries, including industrial chemicals and fertilizers, but most heavily oriented toward petroleum production and refining together with natural gas production.

Through the subsidiaries of E.N.I. and the subsidiaries of the subholding companies of I.R.I., the Italian government occupies an important role in a considerable number of manufacturing industries. Its share of output in important industries is indicated by the following less than complete listing:

20. E. Calcatierra et al., "The Main Outlines and Evolutionary Trends of the Structure of the Italian Economy," in *Economic Systems of the West*, ed. R. Frei, Vol. II (Tübingen, 1959).

International Differences in Industrial Structure

Industries	Percentage of Output Supplied by Governmentally Controlled Firms
Shipbuilding	67
Tractors and farm machinery	67
Steel[21]	38
Motors and engines	33
Aircraft	22
Petroleum refining[22]	21
Railway rolling stock	20
Cement	11
Passenger automobiles[23]	10
Trucks[23]	9

This tabulation does not cover the extent of government participation in the following industries in which it produces: electrical machinery, industrial machinery, textile machinery, machine tools, miscellaneous metal fabrication, optical products, industrial chemicals, and electronic equipment. The government is the largest single producer in the steel, shipbuilding, tractor, and farm machinery industries, and the dominant producer in all of these but steel. Otherwise it is generally one of the principal producers but not the largest in the various industries within which it operates.

In general, except in the few industries dominated by the government, state-controlled firms compete with private firms for a profit, though the government has subsidized operations in shipbuilding, shipping, and some "engineering" industries, partly from the profits of its operations in other industries. Whether or not or to what extent the presence of

21. Government enterprise controls 57 per cent of national open-hearth steelmaking capacity.
22. Most of E.N.I. participation in petroleum refining rests on a 50–50 holding of its largest refinery with Standard Oil Company of New Jersey, and on a 51–49 holding of its second largest refinery with British Petroleum Company.
23. The government firm is the second largest in the Italian motor vehicle industry.

nondominant government firms in numerous industries alters the sort of competition and market performance which would otherwise emerge from the observed patterns of seller concentration is not clear, nor is it clear whether the government uses its firms in the numerous industries in question to influence or control pricing, output, and investment policies. The Italian government clearly has a substantial potential leverage along this line, but whether it does otherwise than go along with the quasi-monopolistic policies of the concentrated oligopolies of which it is a member is not clear. The general character of its policy is such that it would not be expected to employ public enterprise in manufacturing industries as a means of limiting private monopoly power.

"Super-control" groups as such do not stand out in modern Italy, but there are at least five large diversified private firms each of which has important operations in several industries. Fiat, the largest private company in Italy, is the dominant producer of motor vehicles and an important producer of railway rolling stock, engines, steel, aircraft, machine tools, and refrigerators. Montecatini, the third largest private concern (Shell Oil is the second), is the largest producer of nonferrous metals, including aluminum, and of organic and inorganic chemicals, and also produces synthetic fibers, paints and varnishes, and pharmaceuticals. Its largest output is in industrial chemicals, though it dominates the nonferrous metal field as well and is not unimportant in the other lines. Since the nationalization of electric power, Società Edison produces chemicals and petrochemicals, refined petroleum, steel, electrical equipment, and electronic equipment. Olivetti is a very large producer of typewriters, calculators, and accounting machines, although contemporary news reports suggest that it may soon be acquired by Fiat. Pirelli is an important producer of tires and tubes, electrical cables and conduits, general rubber products, and plastic products.

None of these private multipurpose concerns has the size and sweep of an important Japanese zaibatsu, but the resulting multi-industry operations do provide a basis for inter-industry integration within the firm and for reciprocal dealing, and these things tend to lessen the degree of intraindustry competition which is associated with given degrees of horizontal seller concentration, as does similar interindustry integration by government enterprise.

If top-level seller concentration, super controls, diversified firms, and government participation in enterprise are all taken into account, Japan, France, and Italy all appear as having manufacturing industries in the "modern" sector which are subject to substantially more concentrated control than counterpart industries in the United States and the United Kingdom. Although the institutional bases of control vary considerably among the three countries, all appear in the main as representative of highly concentrated capitalistic economies with either limited socialization of industry or with selective socialization employed cooperatively with private-sector interests. And none has a meaningful anti-monopoly or procompetitive policy.

To return to Italy, import competition again does not appear as an important factor in domestic markets for manufactured goods. Exceptions to this rule include lead, of which 21 per cent of the domestic supply is imported, and the aircraft industry, in which imports account for about 40 per cent of domestic sales.

As some of the products of the very concentrated industries of the United Kingdom, Japan, France, and Italy (and Sweden as well) enter the world export market, effective seller concentration in that market is of course much lower. This is true of world markets for motor vehicles, farm machinery, electrical industrial machinery and other industrial machinery, industrial chemicals, textiles, and so forth. But by and large they are not exposed to much import competition in their domestic markets because of tariffs, other trade restrictions, and various technical and geographical considerations.

102

In Canada we encounter for the first time in our intercountry comparisons a country small enough in population and in size of domestic markets that small size alone can account for a substantially greater degree of seller concentration in manufacturing industries than is found in the United States. This is not true of Japan, France, and Italy, where other explanations must be sought as essential supplements to smaller size.

In Table 4–6 we compare the 22 comparably defined industries in the United States and Canada with respect to top-level seller concentration. The data for the United States refer to 1954 and the value of shipments; those for Canada are based on a 1948 Canadian census and measure market shares in terms of employment. The Canadian concentration ratios were developed from raw census data by Gideon Rosenbluth;[24] unfortunately, the only systematic concentration measure easily comparable to those for other countries refers to proportion of the industry controlled by the three largest firms. (Reviewing available data based on internal censuses in other countries, there seems to have been almost a deliberate effort to avoid developing concentration ratios which would be directly comparable to preexisting ratios for manufacturing industries in the United States. Whether this has to do with national pride or a desire to obfuscate is not clear.)

In 16 of these 22 industries, Canadian top-level concentration is significantly greater than that in counterpart industries in the United States, while in the other 6 industries concentration is slightly less or greater or roughly the same. In differential degree of top-level concentration, Canada appears to fall roughly in a class with Italy.

24. *Concentration in Canadian Manufacturing Industries* (Princeton, N.J., 1957).

TABLE 4–6

Canada and United States—Comparative Percentages of Twenty-two
Industries Controlled by the Largest Firms. 1948 and 1954

PERCENTAGES OF SHIPMENTS OR
EMPLOYMENT CONTROLLED

	United States 1954 Value of Shipments by Largest Firms		Canada 1948 Employment by Largest Firms	
Industries[a]	Four Largest	Eight Largest	Three Largest	Four or More Largest
Primary aluminum	100	—	100[b]	—
Passenger automobiles[c]	98	99	100	—
Soap	85	89	75	—
Cigarettes[d]	82	99	85	—
Trucks[c]	77	93	100	—
Matches	74	93	98	—
Steel ingots	64	76	81	99[e]
Railway cars	64	81	79	98[f]
Distilled liquor	64	79	84	—
Shortening and cooking oils	55	80	54	—
Aircraft	47	76	78	—
Shipbuilding and repairing	43	58	32	—
Flour and meal	40	52	35	—
Petroleum refining[g]	32	48	79	—
Cement	31	48	100	—
Canned and preserved fruits, vegetables	28	39	32	—
Beer and ale	27	41	49	—
Paints and varnishes	27	37	32	—
Pharmaceutical products	25	44	20	—
Hosiery mills	22	31	16	—
Wool yarn	20	32	39	—
Cotton textiles	18	29	60	—

[a]Industry classifications for U.S. are census four-digit industries; for Canada they are similar unless otherwise indicated.
[b]100 per cent control by one firm.
[c]Data refer to 1959; market shares in terms of units of output.
[d]Includes all tobacco products for Canada.
[e]99 per cent controlled by eight firms.
[f]98 per cent controlled by five firms.
[g]Data refer to 1959; market shares in throughput capacity.

Sources: U.S. Senate, *Concentration in American Industry;* Gideon Rosenbluth, *Concentration in Canadian Manufacturing Industry* (Princeton, N.J., 1957); private industry sources, for data on passenger automobile and truck industries.

Comparative Company Concentration

If concentration is measured at a slightly lower level, Canadian manufacturing industries appear even more distinctly to have higher concentration than counterpart industries in the United States. Of all Canadian manufacturing industries, half of them had 80 per cent or more of their employment accounted for by 9 or fewer firms, and one-third of them had 80 per cent of their employment accounted for by 4 or fewer firms.[25] Higher top-level concentration is thus accompanied by a comparative fewness of the total number of firms in most industries. Domination of industries by a single firm in Canada is uncommon; the principal instance involving a private single-firm monopoly is the primary aluminum industry.

There is not much direct government interference with Canadian manufacturing industry. Cartels as such are illegal, and the government is said to follow a policy of "vigorous enforcement"[26] of anticombination laws, in addition to having been in the process of encouraging competition by "lowering" tariffs,[27] though Canada would begin lowering from a position of fairly solid protectionism. It is also suggested that a high degree of foreign ownership of Canadian industry tends to limit competition,[28] though this would apparently tend to be the case mainly to the extent that foreign-owned Canadian producers are also the main marketers of imports in various industries. Competition is also significantly limited by regionalization of some industries (more so than in the United States because the regions are much less populous), a tendency understandable in view of the fact that Canada is about as oversized in geographical area as it is undersized in population.

There is no participation by the Canadian government in

25. O. W. Main, "The Canadian Economy," *Economic Systems of the West*, Vol. II.
26. Ibid.
27. Ibid.
28. Ibid.

manufacturing industries as a producer, and no particular evidence of important "super-control" groups affecting manufacturing. Its economy in general of course still depends heavily on extractive industries. Import competition in its domestic markets for manufactured goods is not as important as might be thought, though somewhat more important than in the other countries examined above. For example, its domestic market for distilled liquors is about 22 per cent supplied by imports; for wood products, 33 per cent; for steel, 26 per cent; for pharmaceuticals, 25 per cent; for glass products, 46 per cent; and for agricultural implements, 68 per cent. Thus import competition, so far as import marketing is not controlled by domestic firms, loosens the hold of concentrated oligopoly in some proportion of Canadian industries.

INDIA COMPARED TO THE UNITED STATES

India, of all the countries in our sample, qualifies rather fully as an economically underdeveloped country in the throes of a great effort to achieve economic growth, in considerable part through modernization and expansion of its manufacturing industries. There are available for India no comprehensive data, based on a census, on seller concentration in manufacturing industries, so that we have had to assemble data on concentration from a variety of scattered sources. As a result, we must depend on a rather thin coverage of Indian manufacturing industries, and also on one in which the traditional cottage industries of India are hardly represented. This omission is more serious in the case of India than in that of Japan or Italy, because a higher proportion of Indian manufacturing employment is found in cottage industries.[29] Special emphasis must thus be placed on the fact that a statistical comparison of India with other countries in

29. See above, pp. 22 to 23.

terms of seller concentration refers almost without exception to "heavy" or "modern" industries which account for a minor fraction of Indian manufacturing employment.

Table 4–7 compares 16 Indian manufacturing industries and counterpart industries in the United States in terms of seller concentration. For this sample of industries, the degree of concentration of control of individual industries by ostensibly independent firms tends to be substantially higher in India than in the United States. Indian concentration is significantly greater in 13 of 16 cases, about the same in one case, and significantly less in two cases (tin cans and flour). Indian concentration is substantially higher both in industries which are highly concentrated in the United States and in those which are only moderately concentrated or relatively unconcentrated in the United States. In the industries sampled in general, we find substantially higher concentration than in the United States, the United Kingdom, or Japan, somewhat higher concentration than in France and Italy, and not too great a difference from Canada in the matter of seller concentration.

The high degree of top-level seller concentration in the sphere of Indian industry examined is reflected in a high incidence of dominant-firm control of individual industries. In 7 of the 16 Indian industries sampled, 100 per cent of the industry is controlled by 4 or fewer firms, and in 4 of these 7 cases, all of the industry is controlled by one or two firms. It must be reemphasized, of course, that this comparison does not reflect at all the fact that in an important segment of traditional industries, India undoubtedly has a much lower degree of seller concentration than any of the other countries studied.

The role of the government in Indian industry is evolving at present, as it applies and adapts to emerging circumstances a scheme involving centralized planning of economic activity and limited or partial socialization of industry. As to socialization, it established in 1956 three categories of industries:

TABLE 4-7

India and United States—Comparative Percentages of Sixteen Industries
Controlled by the Largest Firms, 1960–61 and 1954

PERCENTAGES OF SHIPMENTS, OUTPUT, OR CAPACITY CONTROLLED

Industries[a]	United States 1954 Value of Shipments by Largest Firms		India 1960–61 Output or Capacity by Largest Firms				Measure of Control
	Four Largest	Eight Largest	Single Largest	Two Largest	Three Largest	Four or More Largest	
Primary aluminum	100	—	87	100	—	—	output
Passenger automobiles	98	99	47	83	95	100	output
Locomotives	91	98	n.a.	100	—	—	output
Primary copper	86	n.a.[b]	100	—	—	—	installed capacity
Typewriters	83	99	33	—	87	100[c]	output
Tin cans	80	89	20	—	—	n.a.	output
Matches	74	93	60	—	—	n.a.	output
Tractors	73	88	—	n.a.	100	—	output
Steel ingots	64	76	40	80	n.a.	100[d]	output

Industry						
Shipbuilding and repairing	43	58	100	—	—	output
Flour and meal	40	52	5	12	n.a.	paid up capital
Petroleum refining[e]	32	55	45	92	100[f]	installed capacity
Textile machinery	32	46	23	50	71[g]	licensed capacity
Cement	31	48	42	57	77[h]	installed capacity
Paper and paperboard	19	31	25	56	85[i]	output
Machine tools	19	29	40	65	n.a.	output

[a] Industry classifications for U.S. are census four-digit industries; for India they are similar unless otherwise noted.

[b] Not available.

[c] 100 per cent controlled by four firms.

[d] 100 per cent controlled by six firms.

[e] Data refer to 1959; market shares by throughput capacity.

[f] 100 per cent controlled by four firms.

[g] 71 per cent controlled by five firms.

[h] 77 per cent controlled by eight firms.

[i] 85 per cent controlled by eight firms.

Sources: U.S. Senate, Concentration in American Industry; U.S. Foreign Service Despatch No. 732, Steel Production in India During 1961 (March, 1962); U.S. Foreign Service Despatch No. 172, Aluminum: Third Plan Production Target Upgraded (Nov., 1961); U.S. Foreign Service Despatch No. 568, The Aluminum Industry and Trade in India, 1960 (May, 1960); U.S. Foreign Service Despatch No. 603, Indian Copper Industry (Oct., 1961); U.S. Foreign Service Despatch No. 412, The Indian Cement Industry (Dec., 1961); U.S. Foreign Service Despatch No. 357, Business Machines, India, 1962 (June, 1963); Oil and Gas Journal (March 31 and Dec. 28, 1959); India Ministry of Information, Major Industries in India, New Delhi (1961); Ministry of Commerce and Industry, Report of the Ad Hoc Committee on the Automobile Industry (New Delhi, 1960).

(1) a long list of basic manufacturing, mining, and utility industries in which government was to undertake all future development, allowing expansion of existing private firms therein if in the public interest; (2) another list of basic- and intermediate-product industries in which government was to take the lead in development, with private enterprise playing a supplementary role in expansion; and (3) a residual category of industries to be left to the private sector. In practice since then the government has entered certain industries as a producer (in some cases as the sole producer) but has given considerable scope to private-enterprise expansion and entry in "reserved" industries. Thus in a number of industries some mixture of governmental and private enterprise has been established and maintained.[30] Available statistics indicate the share of government control, generally circa 1960, in the following industries listed in Table 4–7:[31]

Industries	Seller Concentration (from Table 4–7)	Percentage of the Industry Controlled by Government Enterprise
Locomotives	100% by 2 firms	75
Steel	100% by 6 firms	40
Shipbuilding	100% by 1 firm	100
Petroleum refining	100% by 4 firms	34
Machine tools	65% by 2 firms	25

In addition, the government controlled percentages as indicated of the following industries not listed in Table 4–7:[32]

30. U.S. Department of Commerce, Bureau of Foreign Commerce, *Investment in India,* by Celia Herman (Washington, D.C., G.P.O., 1961). See also Daniel Spencer, *India, Mixed Enterprises and Western Business* (The Hague, 1959), for a discussion of mixed enterprise in India on a national and state level.

31. India Ministry of Information and Broadcasting, *India, a Reference Annual, 1961;* U.S. Foreign Service despatches.

32. Ibid., and Celia Herman, *Investment in India.*

Comparative Company Concentration

Industries	*Percentage Controlled by Government Enterprise*
Penicillin	100
DDT	67
Nitrogen fertilizer	90
Aircraft	100
Newsprint	100
Telephones and cables	100

These data suggest that to date the Indian government has not made a broad-scale entry into manufacturing industries, but occupies either an important or a monopoly position in a limited number of strategic industries.

Another aspect of Indian policy is that the government is empowered to regulate the operation and development of 165 "scheduled" industries. It does so first by screening the entry of new enterprises to these industries, under a licensing system. A Licensing Committee makes recommendations concerning the capital structure, location, and so on of the licensee and grants or withholds licenses in accordance with implementation of a central economic plan and in view of existing industry capacity, demand-supply relationships, and the availability of materials and capital equipment. One of its aims is to regulate and direct the diversification of industry. A second governmental power is to "control" the operation of private companies in the scheduled industries by surveillance, investigation, and hearing in the event of substantial declines in the volume or quality of production or of unjustified price increases. After a hearing, it may issue directives regulating production or price, requiring stimulation of development, or prohibiting actions which would reduce production, capacity, or economic value. If such directives are not complied with, it may authorize a receivership of the management of the company involved. More generally, the government is empowered to control the supply, distribution, and pricing of the outputs of scheduled industries, and

111

it has since the war (though not necessarily to the current date in all cases) placed price controls on cement, paper, steel, sugar, and caustic soda.

The system described appears to invoke a sort of comprehensive public utility regulation of private enterprise in a broad range of industries, under the aegis of a national economic plan. This aspect of its control of the economy would appear to be at least as important as its establishment of socialized production, and may well alter the significance for market conduct and performance of observed high degrees of seller concentration in many Indian industries. Just in what way or direction alterations are made in practice is not entirely clear. In addition, the government has extensive control of incorporation of private firms, corporate financing, dividend policies, managerial remuneration, and managing agents (to be discussed below). Of the eight national economies discussed, only that of India appears to be departing very significantly from some version of a predominantly free-enterprise economy.

Turning to super-control groups, in India there is a type of such group unique to the country—the managing agency. Managing agencies have traditionally been partnerships, family institutions, or companies which contract with ostensibly independent firms to promote, finance, and administer these firms, and which typically also have gained at least de facto control of the firms whose agents they become by minority holdings of stock issues with special voting rights. There are very numerous managing agencies in India—3,944 by a recent count—but most of them are small and manage only one firm each. However, some individual agencies have engaged in the control of several or many firms, and have been in a position to operate these firms under a unified control, like the subsidiaries of a holding company. At the time 3,944 agencies were counted, 17 of them controlled ten or more firms each, and the remainder less than ten firms each. Central control groups of consequence are found in this handful of largest agencies; the fact that in 1954 it was estimated that 80 per cent of the corporate assets of India were controlled by all managing agencies is unimpressive in view of the large number of such agencies.[33]

The largest 17 agencies have exercised patterns of control over different firms which reflect both horizontal combination and vertical integration, although the latter is predominant, as in the case of the zaibatsu in Japan. Within the general framework of the managing agency system we must also recognize five principal families, houses, or communities of interest in India, each of which controls one or more large managing agencies as well as smaller ones and holds a financial and industrial empire somewhat after the fashion of the Japanese zaibatsu. These are the most powerful super-control groups in the Indian economy, although we lack a precise measure of their absolute and relative importance.[34] Each of them is important in a number of major industries, and the typical pattern of control features vertical integration.

Data on the 17 largest managing agencies in India in 1954–55 reveal the proportions of certain manufacturing industries controlled by the one, three, and five largest of the 17 largest managing agencies.[35] For industries listed in Table 4–7, recognition of managing-agency control elevates the percentage of the steel industry controlled by one firm from 40 to 51, and the same percentage for the textile machinery industry from 23 to 51, but does not suggest any

33. For a discussion of Indian managing agencies, see Raj K. Nigam, *Managing Agencies in India (First Round; Basic Facts)* Research and Statistics Division, Department of Company Law, Ministry of Commerce and Industry (New Delhi, 1957); S. K. Basu, *The Managing Agency System* (Calcutta, 1958).

34. See R. K. Hazari, "Ownership and Control," in three parts, *Economic Weekly* (Nov. 26, Dec. 3, Dec. 10, 1960). The five principal families referred to are Tata, Birla, Walchand, Dalmia-Jain and Mafattal.

35. Nigam, *Managing Agencies.*

other appreciable changes in top-level concentration. Going beyond the limits of industries listed in Table 4–7, the following data show the percentages of a number of industries controlled by the largest one, three, and five of the 17 largest managing agencies in 1954–55:[36]

	PERCENTAGE CONTROLLED BY MEMBERS OF THE 17 LARGEST MANAGING AGENCIES		
Industries	*Largest agency*	*Largest three*	*Largest five*
Railway equipment	80	84	—
Steel	51	78	79
Textile machinery	51	—	—
Sugar refining	38	—	—
Plastics	37	—	—
Motor vehicles	34	—	—
Rayon	27	—	—
Electrical equipment	18	20	—
Tea	11	21	35
Bicycles	11	—	—
Vegetable oils	9	—	—
Leather products	9	—	—
Cotton mills	4	7	8
Shipbuilding	3	—	—

These data reveal nothing very startling about horizontal concentration other than that managing agencies were principal or important control units in a considerable number of manufacturing industries and that their presence probably did not alter horizontal intraindustry concentration much. The vertical integration within large managing agencies, however, may have tended to lessen competition at various horizontal levels, as in the case of the Japanese zaibatsu.

The present importance of managing agencies as an element in the structure of Indian industry must be interpreted in the light of the following facts. In 1956 the Indian Companies Act restricted future operations of managing agencies in several ways. First, it provided for the elimination of all

36. Ibid.

agency contracts in 1960 unless renewal was approved by the government. Second, it provided that no agency or person should be agent for more than 10 companies after 1960. Third, it limited the remuneration of managing agencies generally to 10 per cent of the net profits of the firms they managed (and to a smaller percentage in some cases) and placed other restrictions on agency remuneration. At the same time the government authorized "secretaries and treasurers" of companies to furnish managerial and administrative services to them, such secretaries and treasurers not to have or exercise control of the companies they served.

Thereafter many managing agencies reconstituted themselves to provide secretary-treasurer service, at least sufficiently that individually they retained a managing-agency relationship to no more than ten firms each. Further, some of them have been in the process of acquiring majority control of fewer firms and becoming parent or holding companies to manufacturing subsidiaries rather than managing agencies. How much difference all of this has made for the de facto pattern of control of Indian industry (given the new government policies of regulation of "scheduled" industries) is not entirely clear to us at present. With respect to the managing agencies there seems to have been more governmental concern, and more legitimate concern, with the income-distribution effects of managing agencies via profit shares reaped from contracting companies and through other compensation, with the treatment of shareholders, and with other financial policies than with the managing agencies as vehicles for restraining competition or creating excessive concentration. The governmental policy in India in any event is not particularly oriented toward lessening or stabilizing concentration, since in theory if not in practice, extensive social control should subvert any adverse tendencies of private monopoly power.

Imports as a source of competition reducing the possible monopoly power of national firms in their domestic markets are somewhat more important in India than in the other countries studied. A less than complete coverage of the 16 industries listed in Table 4–7 shows that imports supply 30 per cent of the Indian domestic market in steel, 40 per cent of that in shipbuilding, 57 per cent of that in aluminum, 93 per cent of that in paper and paperboard, and nearly all of that in machine tools. Foreign competition thus significantly tempers the potential significance of high seller concentration in a significant fraction of Indian manufacturing industries.

SWEDEN COMPARED TO THE UNITED STATES

Comparison of seller concentration in Swedish manufacturing industries with concentration in counterpart industries in other countries is severely hampered by the lack of data on Swedish concentration. As in the cases of France, Italy, and India, there are no Swedish seller concentration data based on a census of manufactures, in spite of the fact that the Swedes are very avid and thoroughgoing census takers. In reporting findings from their censuses, they apparently draw the line at revealing the shares of individual industries controlled by the few largest firms in these industries. Further, although various public and private reports enabled us to construct concentration measures for a fair scattering of manufacturing industries in France, Italy, and India, a prolonged search failed to reveal comparable sources referring to Swedish industry. This deficiency of data may of course be remedied in the future; most of the essential data on seller concentration in Italy, France, and Japan were developed from publications or studies which became avail-.able two or three years after the present study was begun in late 1959.

In any event we rely at present on data secured from a private Swedish source referring to five Swedish industries and from international intelligence reports concerning the petroleum refining and passenger automobile industries, for a total of seven Swedish industries which are compared with counterpart American industries with respect to seller concentration in Table 4–8. For this very limited sample, it is found that six of the seven Swedish industries were significantly more concentrated than counterpart American industries, while the other one had about the same degree of top-level concentration. There was 100 per cent control of the industry by one, three, or four firms in three of the seven

TABLE 4–8

Sweden and United States—Comparative Percentages of Seven Industries
Controlled by the Largest Firms, 1959 and 1954

| | PERCENTAGES OF SHIPMENTS OR SALES CONTROLLED | | | | |
| | United States 1954 Value of Shipments by Largest Firms | | Sweden 1959 Sales by Largest Firms | | |
Industries[a]	Four Largest	Eight Largest	Single Largest	Three Largest	Five Largest
Passenger cars[b]	98	99	100	—	—
Steel ingots	64	76	—	49	66
Flour and meal	40	52	—	85[c]	—
Petroleum refining[d]	32	55	50	100[e]	—
Cement	31	48	80	100	—
Pulp mills	29	42	—	32	41
Paper and paperboard	19	31	—	33	45

[a]Industry classifications for U.S. are census four-digit industries; for Sweden they are similar unless otherwise indicated.
[b]Data refer to 1959; market shares in units of output.
[c]85 per cent controlled by four firms.
[d]Data refer to 1959; market shares in throughput capacity.
[e]100 per cent controlled by four firms.

Sources: U.S. Senate, Concentration in American Industry; private Swedish sources; private industry sources, for data on passenger automobile industry; Oil and Gas Journal (Mar. 31 and Dec. 28, 1959).

cases. So far as one can judge from this sample, Swedish industry is as highly concentrated as that in any of the eight countries studied.

This small sample, however, may not only be less than accurately representative of the more concentrated sector of Swedish industry, but also conceals what is reputed to be a substantially unconcentrated, small-enterprise segment of Swedish industry. Our comparisons here therefore have limitations possibly comparable to those encountered in the cases of Italy and France.

There is little direct interference of government with private manufacturing industry in Sweden, and very little government participation as a producer in manufacturing industries. In Sweden, over 90 per cent of the workers employed in manufacturing, mining, and construction work for private firms. Cartels are traditionally ubiquitous in Sweden. However, under postwar legislation in 1946 and 1953, a system was adopted under which cartels were registered with a governmental agency. The agency gives publicity to their activities and the economic results thereof, and seeks to secure corrections of antisocial cartel practices under the pressure of public opinion. In addition cartels deemed to be harmful to the public interest are forbidden. By 1956, 1,700 Swedish cartels had been registered, and of these 40 per cent were dissolved and 20 per cent modified. A commentator concludes that "it is quite clear that there are now probably no cartels in Sweden which can be said to be harmful to society or which are incompatible with the modern view of competition and limitation of competition. The majority of cartels still existing are not directed toward the impediment of competition but towards taking care of certain general interests of the entrepreneur."[37] Without attempting to interpret this statement, it must be noted that if it were supportable, Sweden would have accomplished a

37. Hugo Hegeland, "The Structure and Functioning of Sweden's Political Economy," in *Economic Systems of the West, 1* (1957), 224.

remarkable overnight revolution in its public policy toward private industry. The impression remains that the competition-limiting effects of high seller concentration in principal industries is still significantly bulwarked by cartelization.

Import competition, however, may tend to undermine domestic monopoly power in some significant fraction of industries. Incomplete data suggest for example that about 83 per cent of the Swedish market in refined petroleum products and from 25 to 30 per cent of the market for passenger automobiles are supplied by imports.

The foregoing analysis of comparative seller concentration in manufacturing industries in the eight countries studied supports several general conclusions.

The first of these rests on the "bare-bone" statistics of top-level seller concentration for a sample of industries in which industries of high seller concentration are significantly over-represented and industries of low concentration are correspondingly underrepresented (the proportion of industries of moderate concentration included being roughly representative of the same proportion for all industries). These statistics suggest that the United States and the United Kingdom more or less share the position of having on the average (and subject to substantial dispersion around the average) the lowest seller concentration within individual industries of the eight countries; that Japan has slightly higher seller concentration on the average than these countries; and that in ascending order France, Italy, Canada, India, and Sweden have on the average progressively higher degrees of seller concentration within individual industries, at least for the sample of industries chosen. The tendency toward higher concentration is marked for the last four countries, and probably sufficient to account per se, other things being equal, for the possession and exercise of greater degrees of monopoly power than exist in the other countries.

119

This impression is reinforced by the finding that as we ascend the concentration ladder past Japan, we find in France, Italy, India, and Sweden a significant minor fraction of industries in which all or almost all industry output is supplied by one, two, or three firms, this phenomenon being very rare in the United States, the United Kingdom, and Japan. In the extreme case of Sweden, the total number of firms in an industry is frequently quite small.

The preceding observations should be tempered, however, by recognition of the fact that the "traditional" industries of France, Italy, and Sweden, and the cottage industries of India and Japan, are barely represented for these countries in the sample of industries studied, and that in such industries these countries have or are thought to have much lower seller concentration than is found in counterpart industries in the United States and the United Kingdom. It might thus be suggested that, in significantly varying degrees, France, Italy, Sweden, India, and Japan tend to have "dual economies" in manufacture, made up of "modern" and traditional or cottage sectors, and that their tendencies toward higher seller concentration are found mainly in industries in their modern sectors.

A further tentative generalization is to the effect that in these countries of distinctly higher seller concentration, with the exception of Canada and possibly of India, as well as in Japan, the stronger monopolistic tendencies inherent in the higher degrees of seller concentration observed appear to be reinforced by government policies condoning cartelization and by the widespread operation of cartels—a circumstance which distinguishes these countries from the United States and from Canada and in large part from the United Kingdom. The restriction of competition would appear further to be reinforced by the existence in several of these countries of super-control entities of the sort that brings a group of vertically related companies in different industries under a single control or influence, and that reduces "horizontal" competition at several industry levels by confining supplier-buyer transactions within a vertically related complex of enterprises. Such a function is performed in significant degree by the zaibatsu in Japan, by the great family combines of India, and by several principal private concerns as well as by a governmental holding company (I.R.I.) in Italy.

Governmental ownership and operation of enterprise is significant, among the countries studied, mainly in Italy and India and to a lesser degree in France. In each case such ownership is not dominant, is selective among industries, and most frequently involves governmental enterprises as suppliers of only fractions of the outputs of the industries in which they engage, the rest of supply in such industries being provided by private enterprises. In none of these cases does it appear that the participation of public enterprise along with private enterprises in an industry is used as a device for limiting monopoly by providing "yardstick" competition, though such enterprises are used, especially in Italy and India, to implement certain goals of national planning.

Selective government ownership of manufacturing enterprise, vertically integrated super-control groups, and policies condoning cartelization—viewed generally and as influences on monopoly and competition—all tend to distinguish the countries mentioned in connection with these phenomena from the United States, Canada, and the United Kingdom. The latter three countries are also distinguished in that all pursue antitrust or comparable procompetitive policies, though such policies are perhaps most vigorous and effective in the United States and least so in the United Kingdom. In the other five countries excepting India, as noted, what amounts to a reverse policy of condoning cartelization prevails.

At the present time, direct governmental control of private enterprise activity in manufacturing appears, among the eight countries studied, to be important mainly in India, where some approximation to utility-type regulation of many

121

or most manufacturing industries seems to be the prevailing policy. In several of the other countries, there has been a transitory and dwindling phase of governmental control of enterprise and its financing directed toward reconstruction following World War II. This has been quite important in Japan, Italy, and France, but is currently of waning importance.

A final summary remark concerns the importance of import competition as a force tempering domestic monopoly power. This force is in general not too important, but it does have a significant incidence in India, Sweden, and Canada (except so far as the importers are also the domestic suppliers). In the other countries, import competition appreciably affects only isolated industries or commodities.

5 COMPARATIVE RELATIONSHIPS OF PLANT TO COMPANY CONCENTRATION

Let us now juxtapose the foregoing analysis of the comparative degrees of seller, firm, or "company" concentration among our eight countries with the description in Chapter 3 of the comparative degrees of plant concentration among the same countries for a somewhat differently composed sample of manufacturing industries. This juxtaposition naturally creates some interest in the relationship of company concentration to plant concentration in various industries in the several countries, and in possible intercountry differences in the relationship of company to plant concentration.

Two questions in particular arise. First, to what extent does an excess of company over plant concentration within individual industries account for or "explain" the observed degrees of company concentration in each of the several countries, or in all the countries as a group so far as generalizations are supportable, as distinct from the extent to which observed company concentration is accounted for or explained by existing degrees of plant concentration in various industries? This question is closely akin to that of the extent to which existing seller concentration in the manufacturing industries in question is probably "justified" by attained economies of large-scale plants, and of the extent to which it must look for "efficiency" justifications in the realm of economies of multiplant firms. Second, to what extent do intercountry differences in the relationship of company to plant concentration, as distinct from intercountry differences in plant concentration, account for or explain observed intercountry differences in company concentration?

The relationship in any industry of company to plant concentration is fully measured or described only by a full comparison of the number and size distribution of firms with the number and size distribution of plants within the industry, augmented by a measure of the extent to which differentials in firm size are accounted for respectively by differentials in the sizes of the plants they control and by the numbers of plants they control. It is not possible to devise any really satisfactory single index-number measure which summarizes the relationship of two related size distributions, particularly when the absolute number of items in each distribution is a matter of importance—although various valiant attempts have been made in this direction—much less an index which simultaneously reflects the relative importance of the two forces bearing on differentials in the size of firms. It is therefore expedient, and in general more revealing, to employ simple index measures which reveal definitely only certain crucial properties of the relationship of company to plant concentration in any industry.

Some obvious indices of this character consist of "ratios of concentration ratios," such as the ratio of the percentage of industry output supplied by the largest four firms in an industry to the percentage of output supplied by the largest four plants in the same industry, and similar ratios referring to largest eight firms and plants, the largest ten or twenty, and so forth. Such "ratios of concentration ratios" might be designated as *"company-plant concentration multiples."* We will employ such multiples below, although because of the severe restriction on the availability of data revealing company concentration except for a very few largest firms, we will confine our attention to company-plant concentration multiples referring either to the four largest firms and plants in each industry (for the United States) or to the three largest firms and plants (for the rest of the countries in general). The measures developed thus refer only to comparative top-level concentration by plants and firms, and do not reveal much of anything about comparative plant and firm concentration at lower levels.

These company-plant concentration multiples may be viewed as rough indicators of the extent of multiplant ownership by the largest firms in any industry. But they are no more than rough indicators. Showing only, for example, the ratio of the percentage of industry output controlled by the three largest firms in an industry to the percentage of that output supplied by the three largest plants, such a multiple provides at best a clue to the probable minimum number of plants controlled on the average by the three largest firms in the industry. It does not reveal (nor do the available data) the relative extents to which the three large firms all are larger respectively by virtue of controlling the larger or largest plants in an industry and by virtue of controlling more plants than smaller rival firms but plants not of greater size. Nor does it reveal differentials in the degree and pattern of multiplant development among the three largest firms. The company-plant concentration multiple should thus be spoken of only loosely as an index of the degree of multiplant development by large firms, as it measures something which though related is not quite the same thing.[1]

1. Ralph L. Nelson (*Concentration in Manufacturing Industries in the United States,* chap. 4) finds that in the United States the largest

SOME INFERENCES FROM PREVIOUS FINDINGS

Let us now return to the two main questions posed at the outset of this section, concerning the extent to which excesses of company over plant concentration explain observed degrees of company concentration, and the extent to which intercountry differences in company-plant concentration multiples account for observed intercountry differences in company concentration. Some light is shed on the second issue by reviewing our findings in the two preceding chapters concerning comparative company concentration and comparative plant concentration among countries, although it is a somewhat indistinct light in view of the facts that plant and company concentration ratios could not be calculated for an identical set of industries and that the plant-concentration ratios and relatives presented referred in any industry to the percentage of control of employment by the twenty largest plants, whereas the company-concentration ratios referred usually to the percentage control of sales or output by the three or four largest firms.

It was found in Chapter 3 that the United Kingdom tended on the average to have appreciably greater plant concentration within a sample of comparable industries than the United States, the median plant-concentration relative for the United Kingdom (at the twenty-plant level) being 131 where United States concentration is taken as 100, though there was a wide dispersion around this central tendency (found also in all the other countries). For a differently

---

firms in most industries tend to have larger individual plants than smaller firms as well as more plants apiece, and that interindustry differences in company concentration are in the larger part explicable by differences in degrees of multiplant development, but makes no definite finding on how close the largest firms come to having the minimum possible number of largest plants necessary to account for their market shares.

composed industry sample, company concentration in the United Kingdom appears to average the same as or slightly lower than in the United States at the three- or four-firm level. These findings taken together furnish some basis for the expectation that the company-plant concentration multiple, or degree of multiplant development by large firms, may on the average be appreciably lower in the United Kingdom than in the United States.

In Japan, the median twenty-plant concentration relative within a sample of comparable industries was found in Chapter 3 to be 109 where United States concentration is taken as 100. For a differently composed sample there is on the average about the same or a slightly greater degree of top-level company concentration (at the three-firm level) in Japan than in the United States, though with substantial variance around this central tendency. These findings would be consistent with the finding on the average of slightly smaller company-plant concentration multiples in Japan than in the United States, though a firm prediction would not be justified since we are dealing with comparative plant concentration at the twenty-plant level and with company concentration at the three- or four-firm level, with nonidentical industry samples.

In Italy, the median twenty-plant concentration relative for a sample of comparable industries was seen in Chapter 3 to be 122 (U.S. plant concentration being 100), whereas company-concentration ratios for three or four firms per industry in a differently composed sample average substantially higher in Italy than in the United States. The general indication is that for Italy company-plant concentration multiples might average about the same as in the United States or a little greater. In France, a median twenty-plant concentration relative of 129 was found in Chapter 3; top-level company concentration is on the average somewhat higher than in the United States, though comparatively a bit less so than in Italy. Again, no significant difference between France and the United States in the matter of company-plant concentration multiples is suggested. For India, the median twenty-plant concentration relative was found in Chapter 3 to be 189, for a sample of only 22 industries, and, for a differently composed sample, company concentration is substantially greater than in the United States in most cases. These findings would be consistent with the existence of no important intercountry differences in the average company-plant concentration multiple.

Both Canada and Sweden were seen in Chapter 3 to tend toward very substantially higher plant concentration than the United States or than the other countries under analysis. Their median twenty-plant concentration relatives (for 14 and 27 industries respectively) were 221 and 234, taking United States plant concentration as 100. Correspondingly, both countries display substantially higher top-level company concentration than the United States in most industries for which comparisons were made, but since the disparity in plant concentration is proportionately greater than that in company concentration, Canada and Sweden might be expected to have appreciably lower company-plant concentration multiples than the United States.

COMPARATIVE COMPANY-PLANT CONCENTRATION MULTIPLES

The preceding rather indirect intercountry comparisons of plant and company concentration have been reviewed because, with the data available, direct intercountry comparisons of company and plant concentration can be made only for smallish samples of industries for the United Kingdom, Japan, and France, and for very small samples for Italy, India, Canada, and Sweden, so that obtainable statistical results cannot be viewed as highly reliable.

A survey of all available data shows that there are only 19 industries for which direct comparisons of company and plant concentration can be made for at least one of the eight countries in addition to the United States, the number of possible comparisons ranging from three in the case of India to seventeen in that of the United Kingdom. For these industries individually it has been possible to compare the four-firm concentration ratio with the four-plant concentration ratio for the United States, and the three-firm concentration ratio with the three-plant concentration ratio for the other seven countries. The meaningfulness of the comparisons made are limited mainly by the facts that plant concentration is generally measured in terms of employment whereas company concentration is measured in terms of another magnitude, usually sales or output; that plant concentration ratios are mean estimates from frequency distribution of plant sizes (see above, pp. 26 to 30) and evidently subject to some random error; and that the dates of reference of plant and company concentration ratios are generally different by a few years or more. The data presented on company-plant concentration multiples should be interpreted accordingly as no better than very rough indicators of the exact magnitudes we would like to estimate.

In Table 5–1 we present for each of the countries in question and for the 19 industries mentioned a listing of intra-country company-concentration ratios at the three- or four-firm level, and in an adjoining column the calculated company-plant concentration multiple at the same level. A survey of this table should give some notion not only of mean tendencies in, but of interindustry dispersions of, company-plant concentration multiples in the several countries.

Some of the information contained in Table 5–1 is summarized in Table 5–2, which shows for each country the percentages of the number of industries analyzed for which the company-plant concentration multiples fall within each of several ranges, as well as the mean multiple for each country and also the mean multiple if the largest multiple is omitted in averaging in the case of each country. The indica-

TABLE 5–1

Company Concentration and Company-Plant Concentration Multiples
for Eight Countries and Nineteen Industries during the 1950s

Industries	United States		United Kingdom		Japan		France	
	Four-Firm Concentration Ratio	Four-Unit Company-Plant Multiple	Three-Firm Concentration Ratio	Three-Unit Company-Plant Multiple	Three-Firm Concentration Ratio	Three-Unit Company-Plant Multiple	Three-Firm Concentration Ratio	Three-Unit Company-Plant Multiple
Electric lamps	93	3.5	56	3.1	65	4.7	—	—
Soap and glycerine	85	4.7	—	—	32	1.7	—	—
Explosives	72	1.6	91[a]	3.6[a]	—	—	—	—
Distilled liquors	64	2.5	73[a]	4.0[a]	—	—	—	—
Steel ingots	64	5.3	32	1.5	52	2.2	41	1.5
Aircraft	47	2.0	47	1.9	—	—	57	3.2
Plastics	47	1.6	51	2.0	—	—	—	—
Shipbuilding	43	1.8	23	1.2	32	1.0	76	3.0
Flour and meal	40	6.7	46	6.1	30	12.0	49	16.0
Petroleum refining	32	10.7	93	2.0	42	1.4	72	3.0
Cement	31	4.5	90	8.1	49	2.7	53	6.0
Pulp mills	29	3.2	—	—	27	1.2	—	—
Canned and preserved fruits, vegetables	28	3.1	21	1.7	—	—	14	2.3
Beer and ale	27	1.7	11	1.6	98	2.3	25[b]	2.0[b]
Paints and varnishes	27	4.5	20	1.8	—	—	—	—
Pharmaceutical products	25	1.2	24	1.4	56	5.6	—	—
Paper and paperboard	19	9.5	19	1.9	30	4.3	14	1.4
Cotton fabrics	18	1.4	4	1.0	8	8.0	—	—
Sawmills and planing mills	7	3.3	5	2.0	—	—	—	—

Industries	Italy Three-Firm Concentration Ratio	Italy Three-Unit Company-Plant Multiple	India Three-Firm Concentration Ratio	India Three-Unit Company-Plant Multiple	Canada Three-Firm Concentration Ratio	Canada Three-Unit Company-Plant Multiple	Sweden Three-Firm Concentration Ratio	Sweden Three-Unit Company-Plant Multiple
Electric lamps	—	—	—	—	—	—	—	—
Soap and glycerine	—	—	—	—	—	—	—	—
Explosives	—	—	—	—	—	—	—	—
Distilled liquors	—	—	—	—	—	—	—	—
Steel ingots	47	1.5	80	4.4	78	1.7	49	1.5
Aircraft	—	—	—	—	—	—	—	—
Plastics	—	—	—	—	—	—	—	—
Shipbuilding	67^c	2.0^c	—	—	—	—	—	—
Flour and meal	40	2.7	—	—	35	3.5	33	1.4
Petroleum refining	—	—	12	7.0	61	1.8	100^d	1.0^d
Cement	46^e	10.0^e	—	—	—	—	80	1.5
Pulp mills	—	—	—	—	—	—	32	2.0
Canned and preserved fruits, vegetables	—	—	—	—	32	2.0	—	—
Beer and ale	—	—	—	—	—	—	—	—
Paints and varnishes	—	—	—	—	—	—	—	—
Pharmaceutical products	—	—	—	—	—	—	—	—
Paper and paperboard	19	1.9	56	1.6	—	—	33	2.5
Cotton fabrics	—	—	—	—	—	—	—	—
Sawmills and planing mills	—	—	—	—	7	1.6	—	—

^{a}Refers to six largest firms and plants.
^{b}Refers to five largest firms and plants.
^{c}Refers to single largest firm and plant.
^{d}Refers to four largest firms and plants.
^{e}Refers to two largest firms and plants.

Sources: Above, Tables 4-2 to 4-8, and estimates of plant concentration based on data in Appendix Tables A-1 to A-8.

tions of Table 5–2 cannot be considered very reliable for Italy, Canada, Sweden, and India because of the very small numbers of industries represented, and not conclusive for any of the countries, but the data are presented for what they are worth.

TABLE 5–2

Percentage Distribution of Company-Plant Concentration Multiples
by Size Classes and Mean Company-Plant Concentration Multiples,
for Each of Eight Countries, from Data in Table 5–1

| Country | No. of Industries | Percentage of Number of Industries with Company-Plant Concentration Multiples of | | | | Mean Multiple | Mean of Multiples Excluding Largest |
		2.0 or less	2.1–4.0	4.1–6.0	over 6.0		
United States	19	37	26	21	16	3.6	3.2
United Kingdom	17	71	17	—	12	2.6	2.3
Japan	12	33	25	25	17	3.9	3.2
France	9	33	44	12	11	4.3	2.8
Italy	5	60	20	—	20	3.6	2.0
India	3	34	—	33	33	4.3	3.0
Canada	5	80	20	—	—	2.0	1.6
Sweden	6	83	17	—	—	1.7	1.5

Source: Table 5–1.

Allowing for aberrations in showings based on very small samples, the data presented in Table 5–2 are generally consistent with expectations outlined in preceding pages concerning the relative sizes of company-plant concentration multiples, or relative degrees of multiplant development by leading firms, as among the eight countries. This is obvious enough to require no further discussion. Tables 5–1 and 5–2 also clearly suggest that in all eight countries except Canada and Sweden (unpopulous countries with small domestic markets) multiplant development by leading firms is on the average a very important factor contributing to observed degrees of top-level seller concentration in manufacturing industries. For five of these countries in general a mean company-plant concentration multiple for the leading three or four firms is typically in the range of from 3 to 4, with the United Kingdom probably placing a bit lower. In the six countries, top-level seller concentration probably tends to be three or four times greater than is required by plant concentration, or than is needed in order to realize economies inherent in the largest existing plants. In this regard, the similarity among the six countries is more striking than their differences. Their most significant differences really lie in the direction of those among absolute plant sizes, which seem to be loosely associated with sizes of domestic markets—for reasons to be considered in the following chapter—and of those in plant concentration.

In Canada and Sweden company-plant concentration multiples appear to be appreciably lower than in the other countries, and plant concentration plays a more important role, relative to multiplant development by leading firms, in explaining existing degrees of top-level seller concentration.

All of these findings are of course quite tentative in view of the limited sample of industries for which comparisons could be made and of related statistical problems, but they suggest avenues for further research.

6 THE RATIONALE OF
STRUCTURAL DIFFERENCES

In the preceding chapters we have made a number
of related comparisons of the industrial structures of eight
countries which differ considerably with respect to degree
of industrialization and economic development, population
and size of domestic markets, and the legal and institutional
environment of business enterprise. Our analyses of comparative industrial structure have centered, for samples of
identically or very similarly defined individual manufacturing industries in the several countries, on: (1) the comparative average absolute sizes of the largest plants in individual
industries; (2) the comparative degree of concentration of
individual industry plant capacity in a relatively small
absolute number of plants; (3) the comparative degree of
efficiency in manufacturing production, so far as this is affected by scale of plant; (4) the comparative degree of control
of individual industry production by a very small absolute
number of firms; and (5) the comparative degree of multi-

plant development by the largest firms in individual industries, especially so far as this is revealed by relationships of company concentration to plant concentration in individual industries.

In making each of these intercountry comparisons, our general procedure has been first to compare all of the eight countries, or as many as available data permitted, with reference to each of a substantial number of individual industries and in the particular respect involved, and second to analyze as a group all individual industry comparisons of countries to discover any apparent central tendencies toward systematic intercountry differences or similarities in that particular respect, as well as the degrees of interindustry variance around such central tendencies. In this summary and conclusion, we will recapitulate our findings on the five matters enumerated above primarily by recalling the central tendencies that have been discovered, reminding the reader that the preceding chapters have shown that around each central tendency, or "average" difference or similarity, there exists a quite substantial interindustry variance.

The statistical comparisons referred to, which comprise the heart of our findings, have been supplemented in the case of the analysis of intercountry differences in seller concentration in Chapter 4 by some discussion of factors other than seller concentration per se which might be expected to influence the degree of monopoly power or the tendency toward monopolistic behavior in the industries of the various countries studied. Such factors include governmental policies toward cartelization, the incidence of the super-control group or holding company which brings firms in a series of vertically related industries under single control or influence, the degree of participation of public enterprises in manufacturing industries, the extent of governmental controls of private industry, and the importance of the competition of imports in domestic markets. Since our general findings on the nature and importance of these influences have already been summarized in the concluding section of Chapter 4, we will not further recapitulate them here.

The present summary is thus confined to our findings concerning central tendencies in intercountry differences or similarities with respect to plant size, plant concentration, efficiency as affected by plant size, seller concentration, and relationship of company to plant concentration. This recapitulation will be followed by a brief discussion of apparent or possible reasons for or explanations of the intercountry differences and similarities observed, or at least of those comparative findings which seem to require an explanation. Such a discussion will necessarily have a fairly high content of ad hoc speculation, since some tendencies observed are perversely contrary to a priori expectations and others are not at all uniquely predictable from a priori theorizing.

RECAPITULATION OF STATISTICAL FINDINGS
AND THEIR ASSOCIATIONS

Our main findings concerning central tendencies in intercountry differences or similarities in the respects enumerated above may be summarized as follows:

1. For a broad and representative sample of manufacturing industries, there is a distinct central tendency (the meaning of which is by no means obliterated by variance around it) for the United States to have larger average plant sizes for a given absolute number of largest plants in most manufacturing industries, and correspondingly for the other seven countries to have plants of substantially smaller scale. The difference is such that the mean scale of the largest twenty plants in a manufacturing industry averages from about 60 to 75 per cent smaller than it is in the United States in all the countries except the United Kingdom and Sweden. The difference is less for the United Kingdom, with mean large-plant sizes averaging only about 22 per cent below plant

sizes in the United States; for Sweden it is much greater, with mean large-plant sizes on the average about 85 per cent below the United States level.[1]

2. For the same industry sample, average plant concentration in the United States is the lowest observed for all eight countries, and correspondingly the average degree of plant concentration is higher in varying degrees in the remaining seven. However, the proportional plant-concentration difference is substantially smaller than the plant-size difference for Japan, Italy, France, and the United Kingdom, at the twenty-plant level averaging only from about 10 to 30 per cent. Only for India, Canada, and Sweden is there an impressive difference in average large-plant concentration, the mean relative plant concentration in these countries ranging from about 90 to 135 per cent above that of the United States. Moreover the central tendencies toward somewhat higher plant concentration in Japan, Italy, France, and the United Kingdom are practically overwhelmed by the very large dispersion of comparative individual industry plant concentrations around the central tendencies for these countries, with a fairly high incidence in each case of individual industries with lower plant concentration than is found in the United States.[2]

This finding, which on a priori grounds would seem to have been contraindicated, is of course explicable by the fact that these countries have substantially smaller average sizes of largest plants in the same industries than does the United States. Consistently, the average plant-concentration difference from the United States is largest among these four countries for the nation with the smallest plant-size differential. In general it may be said that the smaller domestic markets in these four countries (as compared to United States markets) failed to be matched with proportionally greater plant concentration because in these countries average plant sizes have

1. See above, Table 3–3, p. 39.
2. See above, Table 3–5, p. 47.

developed as positively associated with market sizes, on the average declining with market sizes though somewhat less than proportionally. In India, Canada, and Sweden a tendency toward much smaller average plant sizes has severely mitigated the tendency toward much higher average plant concentration than that in the United States, but their markets for manufactured goods are sufficiently small that a substantial excess in average plant concentration over that of the United States still remains.

One inference which may be drawn from these findings is that in Japan, Italy, France, and the United Kingdom higher plant concentration than that found in the United States fails to provide a technical basis for very much higher company concentration (only for very moderately higher such concentration). In India, Canada, and Sweden, on the other hand, higher average plant concentration provides a technical basis for much higher company concentration.

3. For a somewhat differently composed sample of industries, the following appeared with respect to comparative seller or company concentration. The United Kingdom and Japan appear on the average, and subject to an appreciable dispersion around the central tendency, to have about the same degree of top-level seller concentration as the United States, with the United Kingdom perhaps falling slightly below and Japan slightly above the seller concentration level of the United States. As for the other countries, France evidences moderately higher company concentration on the average, and Italy, Canada, India, and Sweden still higher company concentration (ascending in the order the countries are listed). Canada, India, and Sweden all have very much higher seller concentration on the average than does the United States.[3]

This finding for the latter three countries is consistent with their substantially higher degrees of plant concentra-

3. See above, pp. 76 to 119.

tion, and with their small markets. The rankings with respect to company concentration of the United Kingdom, Japan, France, and Italy however are not consistent with their rankings in terms of plant concentration. They have just been listed in ascending order of average company concentration. In ascending order of plant concentration they must be listed as Japan, Italy, France, and the United Kingdom.[4] This discrepancy, so far as it is accurately reflected by our data (and it may not be entirely so, particularly because the industry samples used to calculate plant and company concentration differed) should be explained by intercountry differences in the degree of multiplant development by large firms, to which we will turn in a moment.

One thing to note, however, is that although the observed intercountry differences in company concentration—and particularly those involving the United States, United Kingdom, Japan, France, and Italy—are appreciable, they are really quite moderate as compared to possibilities which would be technologically feasible and at least as economical as the differences we observe. In the search for the differences among countries in seller concentration, the slight to moderate character of departures from uniformity (except for India, Canada, and Sweden—and even there the differences could be bigger) should not be overlooked.

As noted in the last section of Chapter 4, the preceding characterization of comparative company concentration among countries is based on a sample of industries in which the "traditional-industry" or "cottage-industry" sectors of France, Italy, Sweden, India, and Japan are barely represented. Therefore, the conclusions just recited should be construed as referring entirely or primarily to the "modern industry" sectors of the countries in question, as they may or do have much lower concentration than the United States in the neglected sectors.

4. See above, Table 3–5, p. 47.

4. A study of the relationship of company concentration to plant concentration, by industries in the various countries, has produced results which should not be viewed as highly reliable because of the generally small industry coverage which available data permitted and the very small coverage for five countries. In this study, company-plant concentration multiples were taken as rough indices of degrees of multiplant development in individual industries for various countries, and mean multiples were calculated for countries.

The findings suggest that company-plant concentration multiples, though widely dispersed, are on the average highest and roughly the same in the United States, Japan, France, Italy, and India, with a modal value in the neighborhood of 3.5 (which would imply that on the average, top-level company concentration is 3.5 times higher than top-level plant concentration as calculated for the largest three or four firms and plants). This finding is roughly consistent with the finding that Japan had about the same or slightly greater average company concentration than the United States, that France, Italy, and India had progressively higher average degrees of company concentration, and that the intercountry differences in average company concentration were consistent with and accounted for roughly by corresponding intercountry differences in plant concentration. Conversely, differentials among countries in the degree of multiplant development of large firms were not a primary factor in explaining average intercountry differences in company concentration.

The United Kingdom evidences a significantly lower average company-plant concentration multiple than the United States (again with a large dispersion around the central tendency) and apparently about enough lower to reconcile the findings that the United Kingdom had on the average significantly a higher degree of plant concentration than the United States but approximately the same degree of company concentration. Canada and Sweden appear with average company-plant concentration multiples substantially lower than that of the United States, and this fact tends to keep the company-concentration ratios implied by their very high plant-concentration ratios from being relatively any higher than they are.[5]

5. The preceding findings refer to intercountry comparisons of plant and company size and concentration in their various aspects. A by-product of our investigation of plant sizes was a set of estimates, based on several heroic and somewhat chancy assumptions, of the proportions of workers employed in the manufacturing industries of the eight countries which worked in plants of reasonably efficient scales. Our tentative findings as based on these assumptions were that in all the countries with substantially smaller average plant sizes (of the largest plants in individual industries) than the United States—that is, in all seven others except the United Kingdom—a dominant proportion of industries had a larger proportion of workers employed in inefficiently small plants than did the United States, and that the proportion of workers so employed in inefficient plants in these industries was generally in the neighborhood of 80 per cent greater than the proportion so employed in the United States, generally exceeding 50 per cent of the work force in the predominant share of foreign industries so affected. In the United Kingdom, such comparative inefficiency affected only about one-third of the industries sampled and a somewhat smaller fraction of the workers in the affected industries.

If this finding is correct or approximately so, it makes much more difficult the explanation of the tendency toward very much smaller manufacturing plants in all but one of the foreign countries as compared to the United States, since we are asked to explain not only small plants per se but a systematic tendency to produce a majority of manufacturing output with inefficiently small plants. Correspondingly, it would be suggested that in six of the seven foreign countries

5. See above, Table 5–2, p. 132.

a needed rationalization in manufacturing production had by the middle or end of the 1950s somehow failed to come about. This finding will thus come in for some further discussion as we turn to consider explanations of, or speculate concerning reasons for, the character of various of our findings.

Once a number of findings have been set down concerning differences and similarities among several countries with respect to industrial structure, there is likely to be some call from the reader for, or even urge on the part of the author to develop, some systematic explanations of the divergences and uniformities among countries that have been observed. In the present instance, this takes on the aspect of a siren's call. For really to develop an explanation or adequate set of hypotheses, one would begin perhaps with a full explanation of why the manufacturing sector of the United States had assumed its particular structural characteristics as regards sizes of plants, plant concentration, company concentration, and development of multiplant firms in numerous industries or types of industries—a task which would fill many more pages than this book so far contains—and then continue by considering how this explanation might be modified in each of the other countries in the light of mutations in type of government, legal framework, traditional institutions, stage of economic development, export-import position, and so forth.

This is a task which we respectfully, and with apologies to the reader who would like to see a book on the subject, decline. Explanations of how, why, and subject to what interplay of forces the manufacturing sector of the United States has evolved to assume its present structural conformations and has maintained them with surprising stability over the

142

past three decades abound in the literature, and rightly so because the subject is a big one. We hopefully assume that most of our readers have a general knowledge of this literature and thus perhaps already have available at least some germinal theory of the evolution and determination of market structures. Similar treatments in depth of the explanation of the evolution of existing industrial structures in most of the other countries we have discussed do not exist, at any rate in organized form, and we are hardly prepared at this juncture to prepare a treatise on the comparative historical development of industrial structures or on a general theory of the development and evolution of such structures. Given this situation, only one procedure in suggesting "explanations" of our findings seems feasible. That is, beginning with the assumption of some general knowledge concerning the reasons for the evolution and present state of industrial structure in the United States, we will confine our attention to probable or possible partial reasons for those observed international differences and uniformities in structure which seem to require any explanation.

The principal uniformities and differences to which we will address our attention are the following:

1. The distinct differences in absolute sizes of principal manufacturing plants that exist between the United States on the one hand and all of the other seven countries studied on the other, particularly as construed in the light of strong tentative indications that inferior plant sizes abroad seem to be associated with the production of significantly larger shares of industry outputs in plants of inefficiently small scale.

2. The less distinct differences as between the United States and the other countries with respect to plant concentration, with appropriate distinctions being drawn between countries with very small domestic markets and those with markets which, though smaller than their counterparts in the United States, are nonetheless moderately large.

3. The counterposed degrees of similarity and difference among countries with respect to company concentration in various industries, with special attention to:

a. The probable reasons why these differences in general seem to stem mostly from differences in plant concentration and very little from differences in degree of multiplant development of large firms, and why, correspondingly, there has not been in several seemingly favorable foreign situations the development of higher company-plant concentration multiples through mergers or acquisitions.

b. The special explanations which are applicable to small countries.

It will be apparent at a glance that the problems presented under the first and third categories are the more difficult.

PLANT SIZE AND EFFICIENCY DIFFERENTIALS

In the whole range of issues with which we are concerned here, comparative plant size turns out to be of crucial importance. Not only is it true that it is with respect to plant size that intercountry differentials are by far the largest, but plant size together with market size determines plant concentration, and differentials in plant concentration in turn seem to play the dominant role in determining comparative company concentration, in a context wherein differences in degree of multiplant development of firms play a relatively minor role. Moreover, the observed intercountry differentials in plant size are the most difficult of all such differentials to explain, if we accept as fact our tentative findings that the much smaller plant sizes found in all but one country outside the United States are associated with a substantially higher proportion of industry outputs coming from plants of inefficiently small size. Why is it that in six of seven foreign countries the average plant size of the largest twenty plants in individual industries is only from 13 to 40 per cent as great as it is in comparable industries in the United States? And why in particular does this hold if its concomitant is producing in these countries over half of most industry outputs in plants with significant diseconomies of small scale? Some significant failures both in competitive forces and in profit-seeking motives as prime movers in concentrating the bulk of industry outputs in plants of reasonably efficient size would seem to be suggested.

A possible explanation, of course, is that our finding of a widespread incidence of production in inefficiently small plants in all the foreign countries except the United Kingdom is in error, and erroneous largely because the minimum optimal scales of plants in the foreign countries in question tend to be smaller in many or most industries. This could be the case mainly because thin and geographically dispersed markets make smaller plants more or equally efficient once delivery costs are taken into account, or because the high relative price of capital goods shuts out the use of specialized capital goods on which economies of larger-scale plants rest. (Simple failure to adopt modern production techniques when they are available and not priced out of the market, together with producing at small scales which are optimal only for retarded techniques, still results in irrational inefficiency.) If it were the case, much smaller plant sizes and virtually much reduced plant concentration would be explicable as consistent with profit seeking by enterprise and a reasonable operation of competitive forces. We have examined this possible explanation however in Chapter 3,[6] and have concluded that whereas it is not totally implausible, neither is it very strongly convincing as an explanation of the much smaller plant scales encountered on the average in six of our seven foreign countries. Supposing that this rationalization of the large intercountry differential in plant

6. Above, pp. 58 to 60.

sizes is not supportable, or explains only a minor fraction of the differential observed, what other explanations can be offered?

The following very tentative hypotheses are offered, partly on the basis of analyses of large plants and of inefficient fringes of small plants in industries in the United States, and partly on the basis of speculations concerning the influences of institutional differences among countries.

1. Some small part of the intercountry size differential (but not the efficiency differential) in at least some of the industries sampled is probably attributable to the established fact that, with broad and deep markets, a very few of the largest plants in a number of industries in the United States are well above minimum optimal scale, though without net loss of efficiency, and to the probability that this phenomenon is relatively rare abroad.

2. In industries in which plant scale curves are slowly rising short of minimum optimal scale, a greater geographical dispersion and thinness of the market in some of the foreign countries may make reasonably efficient plant scales smaller than they are in the United States, once delivery costs are accounted for. This would apply however only to some fraction of industries, then mainly to a very few countries, and mostly to Canada.

3. In some band of industries, but a limited one in our sample, the foreign industries may not actually be producing the same products as those produced in counterpart industries in the United States—in the sense, for example, that handmade instead of machinemade products are supplied. This would blur any direct efficiency comparison by introducing different production functions, except so far as handmaking is a function of lassitude in adopting better techniques rather than a response to expressed consumer preferences.

4. Coming down to somewhat harder and possibly more convincing hypotheses, cartelization or its equivalent in all

the foreign countries except Canada, the United Kingdom, and possibly India may be performing its historically typical function of controlling or dividing markets in such a way as to create havens for inefficiently small or technologically lagging plants in various industries. This tendency would be consistent with the proposition that the cartel is constitutionally an indifferent instrument for rationalization of industry, but is viable as a device for limiting competition mainly if it reserves market shares for inefficiently small plants and sets prices to cover their costs. If this is true, cartels both ease the pressure for rationalization and perpetuate small, inefficient plants by allotting them market shares too small to permit optimally efficient production. In the United States we do find smaller inefficient fringes of small plants in most industries, but lacking effective cartelization these fringes tend to assume lesser importance.

5. We must also consider the hypothesis that in many of the foreign countries involved (Canada and the United Kingdom might be obvious exceptions) there are found generally, and especially as nurtured in markets which are cartelized or not very competitive, some inertia, lack of vigorous enterprise, lack of technological information (ignorance), dampened profit-seeking motivation, and a social resistance to technological change. These things may operate separately or in various combinations to explain the failure of many foreign industries to rationalize production. In spite of outstanding individual enterprises in various industries in the five foreign countries in question, this hypothesis may have some applicability to France, Italy, Japan, Sweden, and India. In India in addition, capricious government licensing practices may be a contributing factor.

6. The existence of privately or state-controlled industrial complexes emphasizing vertical diversification and integration rather than horizontal concentration within the group, as in Japan, India, and Italy, may be accompanied by some shift of attention from optimal efficiency in scale horizontally

to profitable diversification vertically; also, in state-controlled industrial complexes of the vertically diversified sort, cost minimization as a corollary of profit maximization may not be the overriding goal.

For whatever reason, and more probably than not for reasons not consistent with the maintenance of the bulk of manufacturing production in reasonably efficient plants, there exists as a fact a wide disparity in average plant sizes by industries between the United States and six of the seven foreign countries being considered, this disparity varying somewhat among countries. This disparity is in turn one of the bases for a much more modest intercountry disparity in plant concentration by industries, to which we now turn.

PLANT-CONCENTRATION DIFFERENTIALS

The observed intercountry differentials in plant concentration by industries are as we have noted quite moderate as between the United States on the one hand and the United Kingdom, France, Japan, and Italy on the other, with the respective median plant-size relatives for the last four (United States relatives being set at 100), reading 131, 129, 109, and 122, and subject to wide dispersion. This phenomenon is simply the result of the fact that the corresponding median plant-size relatives (78, 39, 34, and 29) are so related to the relative sizes of the domestic industries in these countries that comparative plant concentration ranges from only slightly higher in the case of Japan to about 30 per cent higher in that of the United Kingdom. There is evidently something much less than a perfect correlation between average plant sizes and the average sizes of industrial markets among countries, as the disparity in average plant-concentration ratios indicates, and also a tendency for average plant sizes by countries to decline somewhat less than proportionally with the decline in the sizes of their markets. Among individual industries compared internationally, there is practically no systematic association of comparative plant size and comparative market size, as the very wide dispersion of the plant-concentration relatives of any one nation for individual industries around any central tendency adequately reveals.[7] No very pregnant general hypotheses have occurred to us which would explain the rather erratic association of comparative plant sizes to comparative market sizes among individual industries in any country, though there must be some explanation for anything.

The higher average plant-concentration relatives for India, Canada, and Sweden (189, 221, and 234) are attained even though the corresponding plant-size relatives are smaller than in the four countries just discussed, and much smaller in the case of Sweden (they are 26, 28, and 13). Very evidently, plant sizes in these countries are reduced less than proportionally with the difference in the sizes of their markets, and sufficiently less that plant concentration is on the average substantially higher than in the United States.

COMPARATIVE COMPANY CONCENTRATION

We have noted at the beginning of this chapter, and subsequently, that intercountry differences in average company concentration are "explained" mainly by differences in average plant concentration (the latter in turn being determined largely by plant-size differentials in the context of varying market sizes), and are explained in much lesser degree on the average by intercountry differences in company-plant concentration multiples (or in degrees of multiplant development of large firms). In particular, the mean company-plant concentration multiples for the United States, United Kingdom, Japan, France, Italy, and India really differed rather slightly, falling generally in a range from 3 to

7. See above, Table 3–5, p. 47.

4 with the United Kingdom having a slightly smaller mean ratio. It should of course be emphasized that these central tendencies in the multiples are in each case surrounded by a rather wide dispersion of multiples for individual industries, and that this dispersion perhaps qualifies the significance of the relative uniformity of the average multiple among countries.

Still, this average uniformity and the relative weakness of intercountry differences in company-plant concentration multiples as a force inducing intercountry differences in company concentration seem to require explanation. The conformation of company concentration by industries found in the United States, which is importantly conditioned by a high incidence of from a little to much multiplant development by the largest firms, has been generally accounted for by the dynamic interplay of certain concentration-increasing and concentration-decreasing forces. Predominant among concentration-increasing forces are the drive to increase profits by reducing competition through concentrated market control, pursuit of the advantages of nationwide sales promotion (which may require a branch-plant system in some industries), exploitation of barriers to entry created by resource and patent control and sometimes by product-differentiation advantages, and the desire to exploit economies of large-scale plant. All but the last drive may be fulfilled by mergers and acquisitions resulting in the progressive development of multiplant firms. Opposed to these influences are certain concentration-decreasing forces, in particular the growth of markets in situations in which new entry or the rapid expansion of small firms is not severely impeded, the existence and enforcement of the American antitrust laws, which generally operate to discourage the development of near monopolies and the merger of substantial competing firms but to tolerate oligopolistic market structures, and the fact that the desires of potential participants in mergers to retain their sovereignty, together with a certain incidence of difficulties in arriving at mutually satisfactory merger terms, abort the formation of many concentration-increasing mergers which might otherwise take place. Theories have been advanced to the effect that the historical interplay of these countervailing forces serves to explain the American evolution of company concentration and of multiplant firms, as well as the relative stability in company-concentration patterns in the United States in the last thirty years.

Now this theory or set of hypotheses is reasonably exportable to any of the other seven countries under study. In some instances, however, we would expect it to get damaged in shipping, sufficiently in some cases that much higher degrees of company concentration along with substantially more accentuated multiplant development would be predicted for some of the foreign countries. In particular we might expect that in countries with no strong antimonopoly tradition or policy, including France, Italy, Japan, Sweden, and (in diminished degree) the United Kingdom, the absence of the antitrust barrier to monopolization would weaken concentration-decreasing forces sufficiently that much higher degrees of concentration accomplished by merger and multiplant development by large firms would tend to emerge. Yet they have not done so on the average, since intercountry differences in company concentration seem to be on the average explained largely by plant-concentration differentials.

We are really more or less at a loss to explain in any general and self-convincing way the failure of these anticipated intercountry differences to develop. It is probably true that a very detailed study of institutional and other circumstances in individual countries would be required to provide an explanation. Thus, the best we can do at this point is to toss out a few speculative hypotheses, as follows.

1. Students of the early American merger movement of the period following 1890 and of comparable developments abroad have suggested that the foreclosure of cartelization as an effective device for restricting competition in the United

States encouraged concentration by merger as an alternative device and resulted in at least an earlier development of highly concentrated industries in this country than in industrialized countries abroad. In fact, the interpretation of the Sherman Act from 1890 to 1905 has been considered as a factor definitely encouraging the American merger movement. Extending this reasoning, it may well be true that the extra impetus given to concentration-by-merger in the United States by the prohibition of cartelization has resulted in net concentration-increasing forces at home as strong as those which prevail even in the absence of antimonopoly policies abroad.

2. Given the fact that legal restraints against increases in company concentration by merger resulting in multiplant firm development are stronger in the United States than abroad, the opportunities for multiplant development are greater (without this development necessarily resulting in greater seller concentration) because markets are broader geographically and deeper in purchasing power. The latter considerations may tend in the United States to counterbalance any virtual tendency to lesser multiplant development attributable to a different legal framework.

3. For reasons that are not entirely clear from economic analysis, the great companies or groups of firms controlled by powerful families in Japan, Italy, and India have historically expanded by acquiring diversified sets of plants in vertically related industries (as opposed to moving to monopolize individual industries) in much greater degree than has been true in the United States. This nominally accounts for the fact that the greater degree of multiplant holdings by firms or control groups in these countries is concealed when we count, as we have, only horizontal multiplant holdings in individual industries. It does not really account for the fact that the same companies have not also expanded horizontally to acquire more fully developed multiplant holdings at various horizontal industry levels, unless it is

true (and this is problematical) that they have tended to dissipate their resources in vertical diversification to such an extent that further horizontal expansion has not been possible. If indeed they have, we find one minor clue to the unexpectedly high incidence of inefficiently small plants in these countries.

4. The preceding hypotheses still leave us with the question of why mergers among these great companies in the countries in question—and in other foreign countries as well —have not been consummated to effect more monopolistic control at various horizontal industry levels. Two explanations for this occur. First, cartelization does quite well as a substitute. Second, with competition thus effectively suppressed, the net drags against such mergers in the form of the desire of each dominant company or group to retain its sovereignty and of difficulties in arriving at mutually satisfactory merger terms may prevail (possible in greater degree than in the United States, where cartelization is not available) sufficiently that multiplant development of firms via merger proceeds no further at various horizontal industry levels than it does in the United States.

The preceding list of speculations is not exhaustive but perhaps exhausting; in any event it contains the major plausible hypotheses we have to advance concerning the reasons for the observed relative uniformity of company-plant concentration multiples among the larger countries studied.

The two smallest countries in our sample—Canada and Sweden—have substantially higher average plant concentration than any of the other countries and also substantially higher company concentration, even though their company-plant concentration multiples are appreciably lower. The reasons for their having plant concentrations as high as they do are readily apparent; the only surprise in fact is that they do not have even higher plant concentration, matched by somewhat larger average plant sizes. The apparent main reason for their having lower company-plant concentration multiples is that with small markets and relatively few plants per industry, the opportunities for multiplant development of firms are less. If existing opportunities have not been pushed to the limit, it is for reasons similar to those advanced for the other countries, and, in Canada, because of a fairly noticeable antimonopoly policy.

AVENUES FOR FURTHER RESEARCH

This volume has assembled and organized a good deal of information on the comparative industrial structures of eight countries, has given this information a sort of broad-brush statistical analysis, and has interpreted the major findings which emerged. In addition it has discussed various institutional peculiarities of the different countries which, along with seller concentration, tend to have a bearing on the probable incidence and extent of exercise of monopoly power by manufacturing enterprises.

Our findings in general however are tentative and based on sketchy evidence, and a great deal of primary research would be needed to develop fuller and more accurate information on the matters covered. It is suggested that intensive investigations in depth of the matters surveyed here, almost necessarily conducted country by country, should produce findings which would be useful and interesting not only to economists concerned with industrial organization but also to students and practitioners in the general area of economic development. The bibliography which follows may be of some assistance to the aspiring scholar if he wishes to pursue the lines of investigation we have opened in this monograph.

The most pressing need for further research in the general area we have entered, however, involves development of measures of the comparative performance of industries in various countries which may be matched with measures of comparative structure. In particular, performance in the dimensions of price-cost relations or excess profit rates and of efficiency fully and broadly considered is in need of measurement for almost any foreign country one can name. In our researches, we arrived at a temporarily impassable barrier in our search for such measures because of the unavailability of adequate data in published documents or from governmental or private sources. Intensive scholarly industry of the on-the-scene type for each of a number of individual countries, however, should bring requisite data to light and finally permit the development of the needed measures of performance. It is hoped that some appreciable fraction of the efforts of our very numerous foreign research, advice, and assistance missions may sometime be devoted to digging out and organizing the needed data in various countries, and that domestic scholarly interest in various highly developed foreign countries may develop with respect to measuring industrial performance sufficiently that private sources or public agencies may be induced to gather and furnish basic data needed for measures of performance.

It would also be very desirable, of course, to extend comparative studies of industrial structure and performance to encompass industries in various sectors other than manufacturing. Considering the state of the data, however, the most attractive avenues for further research at the moment lie within the manufacturing sectors of various countries.

APPENDIXES

APPENDIX TABLE A-1 United States

Size Distribution of Plants in Thirty-four Industries, and Percentages of Industry Workers Employed in Each Size Class in Each Industry (1954)

Industries[a]	Number of Plants	Number of Workers	Size Classes of Plants, by Number of Workers						
			1–19	20–49	50–99	100–249	250–499	500–999	1,000 and above
Steel works and rolling mills	204	482,223			9[b] .1%[b]	16 .6%	32 2.1%	37 5.7%	110 91.5%
Nonferrous metals	104	54,494	15 .2%	—	—	27[c] 7.3%[c]	62[a] 92.5%[d]	—	—
Petroleum refining	409	153,069	93 .5%	69 1.5%	54 2.6%	53 5.4%	74 14.5%	30 13.7%	36 61.8%
Cement	153	39,766	2 .7%	7 1.4%	7 1.7%	56 26.4%	81[a] 69.8%[d]	—	—
Glass products	1,253	187,496	840 3.7%	123 2.8%	82 4.5%	58 6.8%	84 21.0%	30 20.0%	36 41.2%
Motor vehicles and parts	2,185	695,464	1,162 1.2%	319 1.5%	203 2.0%	116 2.8%	146 6.4%	79 7.6%	160 78.5%
Aircraft	1,404	822,461	659 .6%	234 .9%	132 1.1%	82 1.6%	115 4.0%	67 7.7%	115 84.1%
Shipbuilding	1,489	125,345	1,065 4.4%	188 4.6%	79 4.4%	54 7.7%	59 13.4%	21 11.1%	23 54.4%
Agricultural machinery	1,360	139,052	889 3.9%	208 4.8%	103 5.0%	48 5.1%	61 11.9%	19 9.6%	32 59.7%
Electrical industrial equipment	5,820	775,257	2,984 2.5%	896 3.8%	591 5.3%	392 8.0%	535 20.8%	215 20.2%	207 39.4%
Electric light bulbs	66	21,960	13 .5%	5 .8%	5 1.6%	10 9.7%	19 28.6%	14[e] 58.8%[e]	—

Hardware	1,748	128,557	1,084 5.1%	267 6.7%	157 10.6%	98 11.9%	99 22.2%	43e 43.5%e	— —
Explosives	74	32,476	19 .4%	9 .9%	9 2.1%	14 4.9%	10 12.2%	13e 79.5%e	— —
Plastics	206	41,143	79 1.9%	40 3.2%	30 5.0%	15 6.3%	21 14.7%	10e 18.8%	11 50.1%
Paints and varnishes	1,630	70,024	1,005 10.2%	285 13.0%	179 18.0%	78 17.1%	71 25.5%	12e 16.2%e	— —
Drugs	1,371	92,049	972 5.6%	181 6.0%	82 6.1%	50 8.0%	51 18.2%	19 11.9%	16 44.2%
Soap	1,543	46,272	1,251 14.4%	149 10.1%	69 12.2%	26 8.1%	34 21.7%	9 12.3%	5 21.2%
Tobacco products	627	94,852	336 1.6%	56 1.9%	60 4.5%	86 14.5%	47 18.3%	22 16.3%	20 42.9%
Sawmills and planing mills	19,778	321,195	16,598 28.0%	1,893 18.2%	760 16.4%	258 11.7%	233 16.8%	30 6.4%	6 2.5%
Wood containers	1,513	52,295	968 11.8%	274 17.3%	140 20.2%	68 16.6%	57 27.5%	6 6.6%	— —
Pulp mills	252	57,670	40 .8%	29 1.8%	45 5.6%	33 9.4%	68 35.9%	32 36.1%	5 10.4%
Paper and paperboard	589	142,189	15 .3%	95 2.4%	107 5.6%	130 14.7%	179 35.3%	43 21.3%	20 20.4%
Grain products	3,415	109,927	2,288 14.1%	529 15.3%	275 17.2%	135 20.9%	174 23.1%	10 3.2%	4 6.2%
Sugar refining	132	30,165	6 .1%	26 8.8%	20 4.7%	58 29.8%	15 25.5%	7 31.1%	— —
Canned and preserved fruits, vegetables	2,172	148,283	944 4.5%	515 11.3%	346 16.4%	259 27.7%	75 17.0%	26 12.5%	7 10.6%
Seafood (canned, packaged, cured)	613	29,051	305 9.1%	150 17.1%	99 25.0%	29 14.7%	27 24.6%	3e 9.5%e	— —

APPENDIX TABLE A–1 United States *(continued)*

Industries[a]	Number of Plants	Number of Workers	Size Classes of Plants, by Number of Workers						
			1–19	20–49	50–99	100–249	250–499	500–999	1,000 and above
Breweries and malt	346	83,949	46 .6%	76 3.0%	60 5.0%	50 9.7%	75 26.6%	26 21.8%	13 33.3%
Distilled liquor	133	21,505	36 1.5%	29 4.3%	21 6.6%	15 10.4%	19 25.3%	10 29.5%	3 22.4%
Cotton textiles	582	296,193	106 .3%	48 .5%	20 .5%	71 4.0%	136 16.5%	115 26.8%	86 51.4%
Wool textiles	588	87,313	141 1.2%	115 4.4%	77 6.3%	98 18.1%	132 43.2%	18 12.5%	7 14.3%
Knitting mills	3,045	221,344	1,382 4.9%	711 10.3%	456 14.3%	234 18.1%	249 27.6%	52 18.5%	11 6.3%
Leather tanning	579	43,465	281 4.5%	91 6.7%	78 12.7%	58 20.9%	60 36.4%	11[e] 18.8%[e]	— —
Apparel	20,306	972,716	9,398 8.2%	5,812 19.4%	2,866 20.5%	1,106 16.8%	972 24.0%	152[e] 11.1%[e]	— —
Rubber products	1,406	246,518	753 2.3%	211 2.8%	136 4.2%	91 5.3%	109 13.9%	54 13.6%	52 57.9%

[a]*Industry descriptions.* The descriptions of industries are based on the industry classifications contained in the United States Census of Manufactures, 1954. These definitions apply to the industries of the eight countries in this comparison. In those cases where there are differences in industry coverage or general description for the other seven countries, notations have been made in the separate country tables (Tables A–2 to A–8).

The following industry descriptions pertain to those industries whose titles are not sufficiently explanatory of the product or products manufactured.

Nonferrous metals refers to the primary production of copper, lead, zinc, aluminum and a miscellaneous category of nonferrous metals. It excludes secondary nonferrous metal production.

Cement refers to hydraulic cement.

Glass refers to flatglass and pressed and blown glassware.

Motor vehicles includes motor vehicles and parts, trucks, and buses. Auto repair is excluded.

Aircraft includes, in addition to aircraft construction, aircraft engines, propellors, and miscellaneous equipment.

Shipbuilding refers to ship and boat construction and repair.

Agricultural machinery includes tractors and other farm machinery.

Electrical industrial equipment includes motors and generators; transformers; electrical control machinery; wiring devices and supplies; carbon and graphite products; electrical measuring instruments; electrical welding apparatus. Electrical appliances are excluded.

Hardware refers to hand tools and hardware including edge tools, files, handsaws, sawblades, etc.

Paints and varnishes includes, in addition to paints and varnishes, inorganic color pigments, whiting, and fillers.

Drugs refers to drugs and medicines, biological products, medicinal chemicals, and pharmaceutical preparations.

Soap refers, in addition to soap, to glycerine, cleaning and polishing preparations, and sulfonated oils and assistants.

Tobacco includes cigarettes, cigars, chewing and smoking tobacco and also stemming and drying of tobacco.

Wood containers includes fruit and vegetable baskets, rattan and willow ware, cigar boxes, wooden boxes and cooperage.

Grains includes flour and meal, prepared animal feeds, breakfast cereals, flour mixes, and rice milling.

Sugar refining refers to sugarcane and beet-sugar refining.

Canned and preserved fruits, vegetables refers to canning, dehydrating, and freezing of fruits and vegetables.

Breweries and malt includes beer, ale and malt.

Cotton textiles refers to narrow- and broadwoven fabrics. Spinning mills are excluded.

Wool textiles pertains to scouring and combing of wool yarn, preparation of wool yarn, manufacture of woolen and worsted fabrics, and finishing of wool textiles. Carpet manufactures are excluded.

Knitting mills refers to hosiery and knitted garments including outerwear, underwear, gloves, fabrics, and miscellaneous knitwear.

Apparel includes clothing, furnishings, millinery, fur goods, and miscellaneous fabricated textiles.

Rubber includes tires and inner tubes, rubber footwear, reclaimed rubber, and miscellaneous rubber industries.

[b]Refers to size category 0–99.

[c]Refers to 20–249.

[d]Refers to 250 and above.

[e]Refers to 500 and above.

Source: United States Bureau of the Census, Census of Manufactures, 1954, Vol. 1, Summary Statistics (Washington, D.C., 1955). Data include establishments employing one or more persons, other than proprietors or partners of unincorporated firms.

APPENDIX TABLE A–2 United Kingdom

Size Distribution of Plants in Thirty-two Industries, and Percentages of Industry Workers
Employed in Each Size Class in Each Industry (1954)

Industries	Number of Plants	Number of Workers	Size Classes of Plants, by Number of Workers					
			1–49	50–99	100–199	200–499	500–999	1,000 and above
Steel works and rolling mills	443	211,903	145 1.4%	58 2.0%	70 4.7%	80 11.6%	34 10.8%	56 69.5%
Nonferrous metals	848	112,100	582 6.8%	91 5.6%	72 9.0%	45 13.2%	32 19.8%	26 45.6%
Petroleum refining	18	16,352	—	—	—	—	12[a] 23.1%	6 76.9%
Cement[b]	57	12,802	—	—	17[c] 3.8%	9[d] 8.4%	31[e] 87.8%	—
Glass products	736	65,382	582 10.3%	47 4.7%	42 9.3%	27[d] 12.1%	32[f] 38.6%	6[g] 25.0%
Motor vehicles[h] and parts	1,541	379,402	993 3.6%	160 3.0%	151 5.6%	98 8.1%	57 10.8%	82 68.9%
Aircraft[i]	314	241,652	81 .7%	42 1.2%	41 2.5%	55 7.3%	35 10.5%	60 77.8%
Shipbuilding	1,111	220,473	727 4.5%	120 3.9%	89 5.7%	84 11.7%	44 13.4%	47 60.8%
Electrical industrial equipment[j]	1,788	311,424	1,239 5.3%	168 3.9%	143 6.5%	117 12.5%	51 11.7%	70 60.1%

Industry														
Electric light bulbs	176	15,450	103	15.1%	37	16.5%	17	15.3%	13	24.4%	6	28.7%[k]	—	—
Hardware	4,586	212,582	3,771	21.6%	405	13.2%	202	13.4%	131	18.9%	54	17.7%	23	15.2%
Explosives	70	40,662	17	.7%	9	1.5%	14	5.2%	7[l]	5.9%	23[m]	86.7%	—	—
Plastics	81	22,054	34	2.8%	13	4.4%	9	5.9%	9[q]	12.3%	13[n]	48.5%	3	26.1%
Paints and varnishes	625	37,912	463	16.8%	75	14.3%	50	18.1%	20	16.0%	17[k]	34.8%	—	—
Drugs	442	49,276	287	7.6%	49	7.1%	51	14.1%	35	21.8%	12	16.7%	8	32.7%
Soap	229	22,065	180	10.4%	22	7.0%	11	6.8%	6	9.8%	6	24.4%	4	41.6%
Tobacco products	105	41,250	50	2.0%	10	1.6%	7	2.3%	17	15.2%	9	17.2%	12	61.7%
Sawmills and planing mills[o]	5,986	102,428	5,532	47.0%	296	20.0%	92	12.3%	61	17.3%	5[k]	3.4%	—	—
Wood containers	1,204	26,691	1,057	46.3%	100	25.3%	39	20.1%	8[p]	8.3%	—	—	—	—
Paper and paperboard	306	78,194	72	1.8%	62	5.8%	57	10.8%	72	29.8%	33	29.8%	10	22.0%
Grain products	1,058	35,499	892	21.3%	71	13.6%	51	18.8%	38	33.5%	6	12.8%[k]	—	—
Sugar refining[q]	68	18,740	24	1.6%	10	3.8%	6	4.5%	11[l]	16.2%	17[m]	73.9%	—	—

163

APPENDIX TABLE A-2 United Kingdom (continued)

Industries	Number of Plants	Number of Workers	Size Classes of Plants, by Number of Workers					
			1–49	50–99	100–199	200–499	500–999	1,000 and above
Canned and preserved fruits, vegetables	535	53,998	336 8.9%	70 9.4%	58 15.9%	47 24.8%	14^r 14.9%	10^s 26.1%
Seafood (canned, packaged, cured)	392	6,726	366 55.1%	21 22.9%	5^t 22.0%	—	—	—
Breweries and malt	804	68,291	509 12.7%	130 13.6%	79 16.6%	66 30.4%	13 14.0%	7 12.7%
Distilled liquor	113	5,060	94 41.5%	4 5.7%	15^t 52.8%	—	—	—
Cotton textiles	870	104,651	273 6.0%	219 15.5%	218 29.6%	153^u 41.5%	7^s 7.4%	—
Wool textiles	1,947	196,409	992 8.8%	323 11.7%	353 25.3%	230 34.1%	39 12.3%	10 7.8%
Knitting mills	1,419	122,819	861 13.9%	243 14.0%	170 19.5%	109 27.5%	31 17.1%	5 8.0%
Leather tanning	628	31,628	440 22.9%	103 23.0%	59 26.7%	26^u 27.4%	—	—
Apparel	12,202	422,495	10,139 26.7%	1,106 18.1%	577 18.8%	298 20.5%	67 10.3%	15 5.6%
Rubber products	560	106,297	335 3.7%	66 4.4%	52 6.9%	60 17.6%	25 16.8%	22 50.6%

[a] Refers to size category 0–999.
[b] Data pertain to 1958 census figures.
[c] Refers to 0–199.
[d] Refers to 200–399.
[e] Refers to 400 and above.
[f] Refers to 400–1,499.
[g] Refers to 1,500 and above.
[h] Includes bicycles.
[i] Excludes aircraft engines.
[j] Includes electrical equipment for motor vehicles, bicycles, and aircraft.
[k] Refers to 500 and above.

[l] Refers to 200–299.
[m] Refers to 300 and above.
[n] Refers to 400–999.
[o] Includes some finished timber products.
[p] Refers to 200 and above.
[q] Includes glucose manufactures and the production of syrup, treacle, molasses, etc.
[r] Refers to 500–749.
[s] Refers to 750 and above.
[t] Refers to 100 and above.
[u] Refers to 200–749.

Source: United Kingdom Board of Trade, *Report on the Census of Production, 1954* (London, 1958). Data include working proprietors and exclude employees engaged in merchandising. See Table A–1, note a, for industry definitions.

APPENDIX TABLE A–3 Canada

Size Distribution of Plants in Fourteen Industries, and Percentages of Industry Workers
Employed in Each Size Class in Each Industry (1957)

Industries	Number of Plants	Number of Workers	Size Classes of Plants, by Number of Workers						
			1–19	20–49	50–99	100–249	250–499	500–999	1,000 and above
Steel works and rolling mills[a]	545	33,638	—	415[b] 17.2%	51 14.2%	38 18.6%	30 30.9%	11 19.1%	—
Nonferrous metals[c]	180	33,993	—	120[b] 4.0%	16 3.0%	13 4.6%	12 12.5%	11 23.7%	8 52.2%
Petroleum refining	64	11,610	16 1.1%	8 2.6%	11 5.8%	12 14.3%	12 35.9%	5[d] 40.3%	—
Motor vehicles and parts	16	32,542	—	3[b] 1.0%	1 4.2%	12[e] 94.8%	—	—	—
Aircraft	70	41,616	16 .5%	20 1.4%	9 1.6%	4 1.5%	9 6.8%	12[e] 88.2%	—
Electrical industrial equipment	486	81,162	175 2.0%	114 4.0%	69 6.0%	41 7.0%	55 21.5%	21 20.2%	11 39.3%
Tobacco products	49	9,902	21 .7%	5 1.2%	7 5.0%	3 4.3%	7 16.7%	6[d] 72.1%	—
Sawmills and planing mills	6,276	50,033	5,766 40.7%	378 18.5%	75 9.9%	35 9.8%	13 8.1%	9[d] 13.0%	—
Pulp mills	128	63,222	6 .2%	11 .6%	11 1.2%	20 4.6%	29 16.2%	34 38.5%	17 38.7%

166

Grain products	962	11,607	—	925[b] 50.7%	14 9.4%	14 16.8%	9 23.1%	—	—
Canned and preserved fruits, vegetables	430	17,354	215 9.4%	119 19.1%	56 21.5%	32 25.3%	8[f] 24.7%	—	—
Seafood (canned, packaged, cured)	431	13,191	—	366[b] 32.6%	29 16.1%	27 27.5%	9 23.8%	—	—
Apparel	2,550	90,646	1,304 12.0%	754 23.5%	302 22.8%	136 20.2%	45 14.2%	9[d] 7.3%	—
Rubber products	88	22,178	31 .9%	16 1.9%	9 2.9%	7 4.3%	7 9.5%	11 32.4%	7 48.1%

[a]Refers to fabricated structural steel and sheet metal products.

[b]Refers to size category 0–49.

[c]Refers to nonferrous smelting, brass and copper.

[d]Refers to 500 and above.

[e]Refers to 100 and above.

[f]Refers to 250 and above.

Source: Dominion Bureau of Statistics, *General Review of Manufacturing Industries, 1957* (Ottawa, 1960). See Table A–1, note a, for industry definitions.

APPENDIX TABLE A-4 Sweden

Size Distribution of Plants in Twenty-six Industries, and Percentages of Industry Workers Employed in Each Size Class in Each Industry (1957)

Industries	Number of Plants	Number of Workers	Size Classes of Plants, by Number of Workers						
			5–19	20–49	50–99	100–199	200–499	500–999	1,000 and above
Steel works and rolling mills	51	34,021	4 / .1%	8 / .8%	2 / .5%	5 / 1.9%	13 / 13.2%	10 / 21.4%	9 / 62.1%
Nonferrous metals	18	4,893	5 / 1.0%	5 / 3.4%	4 / 6.3%	—	1 / 6.2%	—	3 / 83.1%
Petroleum refining	5	1,797	—	2 / 4.0%	—	2[a] / 40.3%	—	—	1 / 55.7%
Cement	8	1,718	—	1 / 2.4%	—	2 / 20.4%	5 / 77.2%	—	—
Glass products	99	6,138	40 / 4.7%	17 / 9.5%	24 / 29.9%	14 / 32.9%	3 / 13.2%	1 / 9.8%	—
Shipbuilding	135	27,175	87 / 2.2%	16 / 1.8%	12 / 3.1%	5 / 2.5%	5 / 5.9%	3 / 9.0%	7 / 75.5%
Explosives	13	3,118	2 / .7%	2 / 2.3%	3 / 7.4%	2 / 8.7%	2 / 28.3%	1 / 17.4%	1 / 35.2%
Plastics	104	3,624	72 / 17.7%	12 / 10.2%	12 / 24.0%	6 / 21.1%	1 / 6.9%	1 / 20.1%	—
Paints and varnishes	59	1,730	34 / 15.9%	15 / 25.4%	8 / 38.8%	1[b] / 8.2%	1[c] / 11.7%	—	—

Industry		Total													
Drugs	18	1,138	9	5.5%	2	5.0%	2	12.4%	4	43.4%	1	33.7%	—	—	—	—
Tobacco products	8	1,138	—	—	—	—	1	6.0%	4	44.0%	3	50%	—	—	—	—
Sawmills and planing mills	1,113	26,188	824	31.8%	206	23.5%	36	9.0%	29	15.1%	16	16.2%	2	4.4%	—	—
Wood containers	65	998	54	43.2%	7	22.9%	3	23.6%	1	10.3%	—	—	—	—	—	—
Pulp mills	72	20,181	2	.1%	6	1.2%	5	2.2%	21	16.4%	28	41.1%	9	32.5%	1	6.5%
Paper and paperboard	73	21,530	3	.2%	2	.4%	14	5.0%	16	11.3%	26	40.2%	9	28.6%	3	14.3%
Grain products	39	1,428	22	13.4%	8	17.4%	4	17.6%	4	35.5%	1	16.1%	—	—	—	—
Sugar refining	16	2,201	—	—	2	2.5%	6	28.6%	5	28.5%	3	40.4%	—	—	—	—
Canned and preserved fruits, vegetables	128	4,982	69	16.4%	36	27.9%	12	16.2%	10	32.6%	1	6.9%	—	—	—	—
Seafood (canned, packaged, cured)	88	2,512	48	18.6%	27	35.0%	7	17.7%	6	28.7%	—	—	—	—	—	—
Breweries and malt	163	5,104	82	14.1%	54	34.2%	22	30.8%	3	7.9%	2	13.0%	—	—	—	—
Distilled liquor	107	1,261	100	50.8%	3	7.9%	3	19.4%	—	—	1	21.9%	—	—	—	—
Wool textiles	91	9,259	36	2.3%	12	4.1%	16	12.5%	11	17.5%	15	52.3%	—	—	1	11.3%

APPENDIX TABLE A–4 Sweden (continued)

Industries	Number of Plants	Number of Workers	Size Classes of Plants, by Number of Workers						
			5–19	20–49	50–99	100–199	200–499	500–999	1,000 and above
Knitting mills	204	8,941	108 13.1%	50 16.9%	22 18.0%	13 18.2%	11 33.8%	—	—
Leather tanning	29	2,205	9 4.5%	7 9.2%	7 20.3%	2 12.8%	4 53.2%	—	—
Apparel	741	38,944	283 8.9%	261 22.1%	104 18.9%	66 24.8%	24 17.3%	2 3.1%	1 4.9%
Rubber products	34	7,776	14 1.6%	7 3.7%	4 3.5%	1 1.6%	4 15.7%	2 18.5%	2 55.4%

[a]Refers to size category 100–499.
[b]Refers to 100–249.
[c]Refers to 250–499.

Source: Sweden Board of Trade, Industri, 1957 (Stockholm, 1959). Data pertain to establishments employing five or more workers, and include working proprietors. See Table A–1, note a, for industry definitions.

Size Distribution of Plants in Thirty-one Industries, and Percentages of Industry Workers Employed in Each Size Class in Each Industry (1954)

Industries	Number of Plants	Number of Workers	Size Classes of Plants, by Number of Workers						
			1–19	20–49	50–99	100–199	200–499	500–999	1,000 and above
Steel works and rolling mills[a]	190	187,317	44 .2%	17 .3%	11 .5%	23 1.3%	23 3.9%	20 8.0%	52 85.8%
Nonferrous metals	221	16,560	125 4.5%	30 5.2%	14 7.1%	14 11.1%	15 25.0%	7 29.0%	2 18.1%
Petroleum refining	68	20,531	28 .9%	9 1.6%	4 1.3%	1 .7%	6 8.7%	7 31.2%	9 55.6%
Cement	625	24,302	435 9.7%	70 8.8%	30 9.0%	28 18.3%	37 43.2%	4 11.0%	— —
Glass products	2,084	47,522	1,756 12.8%	136 8.5%	30 5.3%	45 13.8%	39 24.8%	18 25.0%	4 9.8%
Motor vehicles and parts	7,589	183,539	6,940 7.9%	250 4.0%	76 3.0%	48 3.6%	44 6.5%	17 5.6%	34 69.4%
Aircraft	337	62,815	167 1.8%	40 2.0%	25 2.7%	20 5.4%	29 15.6%	20 19.8%	18 52.7%
Shipbuilding	1,664	86,988	1,307 5.4%	154 5.7%	67 5.2%	37 5.2%	23 6.9%	6 3.2%	22 68.4%
Agricultural machinery	1,165	33,264	897 13.6%	140 12.8%	42 9.5%	32 12.5%	17 14.2%	5 8.5%	5 28.9%

APPENDIX TABLE A-5 France (continued)

Industries	Number of Plants	Number of Workers	Size Classes of Plants, by Number of Workers						
			1-19	20-49	50-99	100-199	200-499	500-999	1,000 and above
Electrical industrial equipment	5,111	168,470	3,968 8.9%	477 9.0%	180 7.4%	107 8.6%	99 17.8%	36 14.5%	25 33.8%
Electric light bulbs	125	9,413	67 3.5%	25 9.7%	12 9.5%	5 9.2%	8 27.3%	3 23.8%	1 17.0%
Hardware	2,527	91,314	2,247 34.7%	140 5.2%	46 6.4%	24 6.3%	14 6.8%	38 35.6%	2 5.0%
Explosives	155	26,609	72 1.4%	21 2.3%	12 2.9%	11 5.8%	17 25.3%	13 37.5%	5 24.8%
Paints and varnishes	848	15,170	629 20.9%	116 25.7%	37 17.5%	20 18.4%	7 14.1%	1 3.4%	—
Drugs	1,595	34,763	1,129 17.3%	203 18.5%	82 15.9%	59 22.6%	23 19.1%	2 3.6%	1 3.0%
Soap	330	8,109	259 15.7%	35 13.3%	8 8.6%	6 9.6%	7 24.5%	2 15.0%	1 13.3%
Tobacco products	34	10,013	6 .4%	4 1.0%	1 .9%	4 6.5%	8 37.5%	11 53.7%	—
Sawmills and planing mills	24,417	112,780	22,736 42.2%	—	982 27.2%	196 12.4%	78 9.0%	29 7.1%	4 2.1%
Pulp mills	126	17,251	54 1.9%	15 3.2%	15 5.5%	18 15.9%	15 31.3%	6 21.7%	3 20.5%
Paper and paperboard	331	28,988	118 2.8%	67 8.7%	45 11.1%	45 20.5%	41 43.1%	4 9.5%	1 4.3%

Industry									
Grain products	11,631	38,348	11,218 46.6%	196 15.8%	48 9.2%	22 7.4%	19 16.1%	5 4.9%	—
Sugar refining	243	39,112	81 1.6%	23 1.5%	42 7.3%	38 15.1%	37 30.9%	12 24.7%	6 18.9%
Canned and preserved fruits, vegetables	1,013	21,848	79 14.6%	131 18.8%	74 25.5%	32 21.0%	16 20.1%	—	—
Seafood (canned, packaged, cured)	457	14,601	265 10.5%	67 17.1%	64 31.3%	45 37.8%	3 3.3%	—	—
Breweries and malt	585	17,671	372 12.0%	101 18.6%	47 18.0%	33 27.4%	14 21.0%	1 3.0%	—
Distilled liquor[b]	659	13,312	497 20.4%	82 20.2%	24 15.2%	11 10.2%	16 34.0%	—	—
Wool textiles	3,063	140,978	2,220 5.0%	325 8.7%	176 10.4%	160 17.6%	110 28.2%	28 14.5%	12 15.6%
Knitting mills	8,587	90,138	7,549 19.8%	486 18.2%	221 17.0%	77 12.6%	56 17.4%	12 8.9%	3 6.1%
Leather tanning	1,297	27,796	971 16.7%	188 22.7%	54 13.6%	36 17.0%	17 17.9%	5 12.1%	—
Apparel	102,758	317,853	98,048 41.6%	1,940 19.2%	526 11.2%	299 13.3%	127 11.0%	18 3.7%	—
Rubber products	2,466	60,825	2,141 9.2%	117 6.2%	31 3.1%	28 6.1%	34 18.5%	8 7.7%	9 49.2%

[a]Refers to steel and general metallurgy.   [b]Includes aperitifs.

Source: France, Les Établissements industriels, artisanaux et commerciaux en France en 1954 (Paris, 1956). Establishments which have not been designated by size are excluded from the data as given by size classes of plants, but are included in the total numbers of plants by industries; total number of plants thus generally exceeds somewhat the sum of the numbers of plants given by size classes for any industry. See Table A–1, note a, for industry definitions.

APPENDIX TABLE A–6 Italy

Size Distribution of Plants in Thirty-two Industries, and Percentages of Industry Workers Employed in Each Size Class in Each Industry (1951)

Industries	Number of Plants	Number of Workers	Size Classes of Plants, by Number of Workers					
			1–9	10–49	50–99	100–499	500–999	1,000 and above
Steel works and rolling mills	285	25,097	149 4.9%	76 7.9%	17 5.0%	34 27.8%	4 10.4%	5 44.0%
Nonferrous metals	330	25,911	188 2.7%	77 6.9%	19 5.1%	33 31.5%	8 24.2%	5 29.6%
Petroleum refining	61	8,775	24 1.9%	10 3.1%	9 7.8%	12 29.4%	4 31.1%	2 26.7%
Cement	2,032	24,854	1,764 21.8%	172 14.2%	42 12.0%	53 48.7%	1 3.3%	— —
Glass products	1,565	36,042	1,186 16.3%	238 14.8%	68 13.0%	66 41.7%	6 10.1%	1 4.1%
Motor vehicles and parts	408	76,605	178 1.0%	129 3.8%	41 3.6%	37 10.6%	9 8.2%	14 72.8%
Aircraft	22	6,393	7 .5%	6 3.5%	— —	6 18.3%	2 25.9%	1 51.8%
Shipbuilding	77	39,754	19 .2%	22 1.7%	9 1.7%	12 6.0%	2 3.8%	13 86.6%
Agricultural machinery	505	14,704	343 14.1%	105 16.1%	29 13.5%	25 33.8%	2 10.2%	1 12.3%

Industry														
Electric light bulbs	224	6,670	172	13.3%	33	9.9%	7	9.2%	9	24.9%	2	27.2%	1	15.5%
Hardware	874	20,596	525	11.3%	267	28.7%	43	14.6%	35	33.6%	4	11.8%	—	—
Explosives	404	7,535	372	10.9%	20	5.7%	4	3.0%	6	22.2%	1	8.2%	1	50.0%
Plastics	86	4,126	44	4.2%	27	14.2%	7	12.2%	5	25.8%	3	43.6%	—	—
Paints and varnishes	646	8,288	499	21.0%	109	27.5%	22	17.5%	16	34.0%	—	—	—	—
Drugs	967	28,498	628	9.1%	236	18.8%	50	12.3%	44	34.5%	8	18.1%	1	7.2%
Soap	2,207	17,591	1,940	31.1%	207	25.2%	33	13.6%	26	27.1%	1	3.0%	—	—
Tobacco products	710	51,217	437	4.0%	111	5.5%	64	9.0%	71	30.3%	14	18.6%	13	32.6%
Sawmills and planing mills	6,166	32,217	5,607	47.7%	503	32.1%	34	7.8%	21	10.8%	1	1.6%	—	—
Wood containers	6,089	19,868	5,788	57.5%	280	28.7%	12	4.0%	8	6.4%	1	3.4%	—	—
Paper and paperboard	553	40,775	201	2.8%	215	11.6%	59	10.1%	63	41.1%	12	22.4%	3	12.0%
Grain products	21,524	63,382	20,896	66.9%	532	17.8%	62	6.8%	34	8.5%	—	—	—	—
Sugar refining	70	11,756	5	.1%	5	1.2%	13	8.6%	45	72.4%	1	6.6%	1	11.1%

APPENDIX TABLE A-6 Italy (continued)

Industries	Number of Plants	Number of Workers	Size Classes of Plants, by Number of Workers					
			1–9	10–49	50–99	100–499	500–999	1,000 and above
Canned and preserved fruits, vegetables	897	19,743	593 10.5%	212 26.1%	47 17.0%	42 35.2%	2 5.5%	1 5.7%
Seafood (canned, packaged, cured)	498	4,272	433 24.6%	48 24.7%	9 15.0%	8 35.7%	—	—
Breweries and malt	64	4,509	23 2.5%	18 10.8%	8 14.2%	15 72.5%	—	—
Distilled liquor	1,658	15,454	1,340 30.3%	271 37.6%	31 14.7%	16 17.4%	—	—
Cotton textiles	2,282	136,513	1,466 3.0%	422 7.8%	135 7.2%	194 34.0%	47 23.8%	18 24.2%
Wool textiles	2,291	124,646	1,464 3.4%	453 8.8%	139 8.1%	185 38.7%	31 17.6%	19 23.4%
Knitting mills	26,179	84,354	25,408 41.6%	530 14.0%	123 10.3%	109 26.6%	9 7.5%	—
Leather tanning	1,205	18,442	917 17.5%	213 25.2%	45 16.9%	27 28.9%	3 11.5%	—
Apparel	218,455	411,139	216,576 78.6%	1,431 7.4%	269 4.5%	170 7.8%	8 1.3%	1 .4%
Rubber products	1,724	38,507	1,581 8.6%	86 4.9%	20 4.0%	27 17.0%	5 10.2%	5 55.3%

Source: Instituto Centrali di Statistica, *Censimento generale dell' industria e del commercio, 1951* (Rome, 1954). See Table A–1, note a, for industry definitions.

APPENDIX TABLE A-7 Japan

Size Distribution of Plants in Thirty-two Industries, and Percentages of Industry Workers Employed in Each Size Class in Each Industry (1956)

Industries	Number of Plants	Number of Workers	Size Classes of Plants, by Number of Workers						
			1–19	20–49	50–99	100–199	200–499	500–999	1,000 and above
Steel works and rolling mills	73	56,618	—	5 .3%	4 .5%	14 3.3%	20 12.3%	10 12.5%	20 71.1%
Nonferrous metals	2,297	111,330	1,587 10.7%	403 10.8%	157 9.5%	54 6.8%	52 13.2%	22 13.6%	22 35.4%
Petroleum refining	34	10,403	10 1.0%	3 .7%	3[a] 9.8%	—	9 23.0%	9[b] 65.5%	—
Cement	38	18,705	20[c] 34.2%	—	—	—	—	18[b] 65.8%	—
Glass products	2,039	49,822	1,547 15.4%	269 17.4%	146 19.8%	41 11.2%	23 13.5%	9 12.9%	4 9.8%
Motor vehicles and parts	3,330	142,962	2,296 11.5%	610 13.3%	205 9.8%	118 11.6%	64 13.0%	13 6.3%	24 34.5%
Aircraft	18	9,849	5 .7%	5[d] 3.6%	—	—	—	8[b] 95.7%	—
Shipbuilding	3,284	145,762	2,868 7.4%	239 5.1%	72 3.5%	44 4.2%	34 7.9%	27[b] 71.9%	—
Agricultural machinery	1,720	30,137	1,432 27.5%	161 16.0%	70 15.5%	38 17.0%	15 13.8%	4 10.2%	—
Electrical industrial equipment	2,904	135,124	1,905 10.8%	618 14.1%	203 9.9%	105 10.6%	29 6.3%	23 11.4%	21 36.9%

APPENDIX TABLE A-7 Japan (continued)

Industries	Number of Plants	Number of Workers	Size Classes of Plants, by Number of Workers						
			1–19	20–49	50–99	100–199	200–499	500–999	1,000 and above
Electric light bulbs	514	11,469	301 22.3%	68 17.2%	19 12.2%	12 14.1%	114 34.2%	—	—
Hardware	9,377	53,923	8,861 56.0%	380 20.3%	99 12.1%	31 7.7%	6ᵉ 3.9%	—	—
Explosives	30	7,538	4 1.6%	8ᵉ 5.4%	—	6 10.6%	9 32.6%	—	3 49.8%
Paints and varnishes	280	9,186	189 15.5%	51 19.5%	23 17.7%	8 13.9%	3 7.0%	6 26.4%	—
Drugs	1,258	48,344	841 13.1%	236 15.3%	89 12.7%	40 11.6%	22 10.9%	27 25.9%	3 10.6%
Soap	329	12,042	239 13.0%	50 12.6%	19 10.5%	8 9.5%	4 7.6%	9 46.8%	—
Sawmills and planing mills	27,721	273,379	24,299 58.1%	3,022 31.3%	352 8.2%	45 2.0%	3ᵉ .4%	—	—
Wood containers	11,110	44,938	10,749 72.5%	310 19.1%	44 6.2%	7 2.2%	—	—	—
Pulp mills	125	15,112	44 3.8%	47 10.0%	16 9.2%	2 18.1%	16ᵉ 58.9%	—	—
Paper and paperboard	3,511	83,585	2,974 14.4%	273 10.5%	120 10.0%	65 11.1%	45 15.9%	22 18.7%	12 19.4%
Grain products	3,979	34,322	3,627 51.2%	264 22.0%	52 10.0%	30 12.4%	6 4.4%	—	—

Industry	Total														
Sugar refining	215	155	8.0%	29	9.0%	3	2.1%	10	16.2%	15	46.0%	3	18.7%	—	—
Canned and preserved fruits, vegetables	1,806	1,560	31.0%	139	17.2%	59	16.9%	37	21.2%	10	10.9%	1	2.8%	—	—
Seafood (canned, packaged, cured)	18,240	17,316	58.7%	653	15.1%	160	8.5%	76	8.7%	19	3.7%	16	5.3%	—	—
Breweries and malt	13	—		—		—		—		13	100.0%	—		—	
Distilled liquor	632	480	16.2%	62	9.8%	32	11.6%	37	26.4%	12	14.8%	9	21.2%	—	—
Cotton textiles	13,695	11,426	35.3%	1,572	24.0%	440	15.4%	187	12.8%	42	5.3%	28	7.2%	—	—
Wool textiles	3,436	2,585	12.5%	468	10.8%	191	9.8%	78	10.8%	35	4.3%	55	24.2%	24	27.6%
Knitting mills	6,922	5,983	45.1%	726	26.1%	146	11.9%	42	6.4%	13	3.8%	12	6.7%	—	—
Leather tanning	489	375	36.9%	83	23.9%	21	13.4%	5	6.8%	5[e]	19.0%	—		—	
Apparel	15,165	13,466	45.3%	1,228	23.6%	322	13.8%	119	10.4%	30[e]	6.9%	—		—	
Rubber products	1,490	963	6.2%	224	7.7%	117	9.3%	80	12.6%	76	25.8%	20	15.8%	10	22.6%

[a] Refers to size category 50–199.
[b] Refers to 500 and above.
[c] Refers to 1–499.
[d] Refers to 20–499.
[e] Refers to 200 and above.
[f] Refers to 20–99.

Source: Japan Ministry of International Trade Land Industry, Research and Statistics Division, *Census of Manufactures, 1956, Part I, Report by Industries* (Tokyo, 1958). See Table A–1, note a, for industry definitions.

APPENDIX TABLE A-8 India

Size Distribution of Plants in Twenty-two Industries, and Percentages of Industry Workers Employed in Each Size Class in Each Industry (1956)

Industries	Number of Plants	Number of Workers	1–19ª	20–49	50–99	100–249	250–499	500–999	1,000 and above
Steel works and rolling mills	1,055	93,885	332 5.5%	395 14.9%	158 13.8%	122 14.7%	28 10.0%	9 5.5%	11 35.6%
Nonferrous metals	32	6,975	18 3.5%	4 1.4%	1 1.2%	3 6.9%	1 6.6%	2 16.6%	3 63.8%
Petroleum refining	10	2,963	3 1.6%	5 4.0%	—	—	—	1 26.2%	1 68.2%
Glass products	130	24,276	—	30 3.2%	14 4.5%	59 37.4%	17 25.9%	10 29.0%	—
Motor vehicles and parts	847	69,821	286 5.1%	300 13.1%	82 8.6%	145 32.1%	15 7.4%	12 10.9%	7 22.8%
Aircraft	23	6,093	—	—	19 23.2%	—	2 25.1%	2 51.7%	—
Shipbuilding	55	28,427	—	4 .5%	30 6.4%	7 6.1%	—	5 14.6%	9 72.4%
Plastics	164	7,074	67 13.9%	56 23.1%	24 18.7%	12 24.0%	5 20.3%	—	—
Paints and varnishes	91	5,855	30 5.5%	49 31.3%	1 1.4%	7 22.0%	2 13.3%	2 26.5%	—
Soap	77	9,549	15 2.3%	25 12.6%	27 17.9%	4 8.3%	1 3.9%	2 18.8%	3 36.2%

Industry									
Tobacco products[b]	21,773	570,653	20,088 70.4%	636 2.9%	692 10.3%	296 7.8%	29 1.7%	16 2.1%	16 4.8%
Sawmills and planing mills[b]	81,912	1,646,991	81,691 99.2%	176 .5%	31 .1%	10 .09%	3 .07%	1 0.4%	— —
Paper and paperboard[c]	236	27,685	165 11.9%	34 4.3%	8 2.4%	11 6.9%	4 4.9%	7 16.2%	7 53.4%
Grain products[c]	18,402	410,700	17,024 82.9%	860 6.7%	430 7.3%	85 2.8%	2 .1%	1 .2%	— —
Sugar refining[c]	18,784	517,200	18,334 70.9%	300 1.3%	12 .1%	4 .2%	17 .9%	67 11.7%	50 14.9%
Canned and preserved fruits, vegetables	41	2,804	1 .5%	27 29.5%	6 12.4%	4 15.6%	3 42.0%	— —	— —
Breweries and malt[d]	95	5,673	— —	10 5.6%	28 31.1%	13 42.4%	44 20.9%	— —	— —
Wool textiles	73	16,365	7 .5%	28 8.0%	8 4.2%	14 12.3%	7 16.0%	5 17.4%	4 41.6%
Knitting mills	313	10,483	77 9.1%	197 55.0%	32 22.2%	4 4.7%	3 9.0%	— —	— —
Leather tanning	403	20,172	66 5.5%	241 44.4%	51 16.0%	40 26.8%	5 7.3%	— —	— —
Apparel	70	2,447	29 19.8%	39 49.8%	1 3.8%	— —	1 26.6%	— —	— —
Rubber products	169	30,876	28 1.5%	58 5.5%	35 7.9%	29 18.3%	8 18.8%	8 18.2%	3 29.8%

[a] This size category refers primarily to establishments using power with from 10 to 19 workers. In the case of five industries in which household and small-scale plants are quite important (see notes on source below), the column includes estimates of

APPENDIX TABLE A–8 India (continued)

all employment in establishments with fewer than 20 workers, with or without power.

^bSource for establishments employing less than 10 workers with power and 20 workers without power is Dhar and Lydal.

^cSource for small establishments, as defined in note b, is Prasad.

^dIncludes spirit distilling.

Sources: India Planning Commission, Scientific and Technical Manpower and Perspective Planning Division, *Occupational Pattern in Manufacturing Industry, 1956* (New Delhi, 1959), which contains data referring to registered establishments using power and employing 10 or more workers, and not using power and employing 20 or more workers, based on a nationwide sample survey; P. N. Dhar and H. F. Lydal, *Role of Small Enterprises in Indian Manufacturing* (Bombay, 1961); and Kendarnath Prasad, *Technological Choice under Development Planning* (Calcutta, 1963), both of which contain data on those establishments using power and employing less than 10 workers and establishments not using power and employing less than 20 workers, in the grain products, sugar refining, sawmills and planing mills, tobacco products, and paper and paperboard industries only (wherein household and small-scale plants are very important in India). See Table A–1, note a, for industry definitions.

BIBLIOGRAPHY

Note: Emphasis has been placed on sources referring to countries other than the United States and on exotic sources with which the general reader may be unfamiliar.

CANADA

Books and Articles

Bladen, Vincent Wheeler, *An Introduction to Political Economy,* 3d ed., Toronto, University of Toronto Press, 1956.

Brown, George Williams, ed., *Canada,* Berkeley, University of California Press, 1950.

Caves, Richard E., and Holton, Richard H., *The Canadian Economy,* Cambridge, Mass., Harvard University Press, 1959.

Main, O. W., "The Canadian Economy," in *Economic Systems of the West,* ed. R. Frei, Tübingen, J. C. B. Mohr (Paul Siebeck), 2 (1959), 1–24.

———, *The Canadian Nickel Industry,* Toronto, University of Toronto Press, 1955.

Reynolds, Lloyd G., *The Control of Competition in Canada,* Cambridge, Mass., Harvard University Press, 1940.

Rosenbluth, Gideon, *Concentration in Canadian Manufacturing Industries,* National Bureau of Economic Research, Princeton, Princeton University Press, 1957.

Skeoch, L. A., "The Combines Investigation Act," *Canadian Journal of Economics and Political Science, 22* (1956), 17–37.

Stylott, Stefan, "Combines Policy," *Canadian Journal of Economics and Political Science, 22* (1956), 38–45.

Wilson, G. W., "Anti-Combines Policy and Inquiry to the Public," *Canadian Journal of Economics and Political Science, 23* (1957), 121–27.

Wolfe, J. N., "Some Empirical Issues in Canadian Combines Policy," *Canadian Journal of Economics and Political Science,* *23* (1957), 113–21.

Government Publications

Department of Justice, Report of the Commissioner, Combines Investigation Act, *Canada and International Cartels,* Ottawa, King's Printer, 1945.

Dominion Bureau of Statistics, *General Review of the Manufacturing Industries of Canada, 1957,* Ottawa, Queen's Printer, 1960.

———, *Iron and Steel Review, 1957,* Ottawa, Queen's Printer, 1960.

———, *Type of Ownership and Size of Establishment Engaged in Manufacture in Canada, 1957,* Ottawa, Queen's Printer, 1958.

Royal Commission on Canada's Economic Prospects, *Canada-United States Economic Relations,* by Irving Brecher and S. S. Reisman, Ottawa, E. Cloutier, 1957.

———, *The Canadian Chemical Industry,* by John Davis, Ottawa, E. Cloutier, 1957.

———, *Canadian Economic Growth and Development from 1939–1955,* by J. M. Smith, Ottawa, E. Cloutier, 1957.

———, *Canadian Secondary Manufacturing Industry,* by D. H. Fullerton and H. A. Hampson, Ottawa, E. Cloutier, 1957.

———, *Final Report, November 1957,* Ottawa, E. Cloutier, 1958.

———, *Industrial Concentration,* by the Canadian Bank of Commerce, Ottawa, E. Cloutier, 1956.

FRANCE

Books and Articles

L'Argus de l'Automobile et des Locomotions, *Statistiques automobiles, 1958,* Paris, June 11, 1959.

Baum, Warren, *The French Economy and the State,* Rand Corporation Research Study, Princeton, Princeton University Press, 1958.

Capronnier, François, *La Crise de l'industrie cotonnière Française,* Paris, Editions Genin, 1959.

Entreprise, "Les 500 Premières Sociétés françaises," Paris, No. 316, Sept. 23, 1961.

Goetz-Girey, Robert, "Monopoly and Competition in France," in *Monopoly and Competition and Their Regulation,* ed. Edward Chamberlin (London, Macmillan, 1954), pp. 21–42.

Hackett, John, and Hackett, Anne Marie, *Economic Planning in France,* London, Allen and Unwin, 1963.

Houssiaux, Jacques, *Le Pouvoir de monopole,* Paris, Sirey, 1958.

Les Informations industrielles et commerciales, Feb. 23, March 2, 9, 15, 23, and 30, 1962.

Sheahan, John, *Promotion and Control of Industry in Postwar France,* Cambridge, Mass., Harvard University Press, 1963.

U. S. Department of State, Foreign Service despatches pertaining to a number of industries during 1960–64.

L'Usine nouvelle, Paris, Société de Périodiques Techniques et Industrielles, 1961.

La Vie française, Paris, March and April 1962.

Government Publications

Institut National de la Statistique et des Études Économiques, *Annuaire statistique de la France, 1961,* Paris, Imperimerie Nationale, 1962.

———, *Direction de la conjoncture et des études économiques,* Paris, Presses Universitaires de France (monthly), 1959–62.

———, *Les Établissements industriels, artisanaux et commerciaux en France en 1954,* Paris, Imprimerie Nationale, 1956.

———, *Les Établissements industriels, artisanaux et commerciaux en France en 1958,* Paris, Imprimerie Nationale, 1959.

Ministère des Finances, *Statistiques et études financières,* Paris, Imprimerie Nationale, no. 147, March 1961.

Ministère de l'Industrie et du Commerce, Bureau Central de Statistique Industrielle, *Annuaire de statistique industrielle, 1959,* Paris, Imprimerie Nationale, 1960.

———, Direction des Industries Chemiques, *Rapport sur l'activité des industries chemiques en 1958,* Paris, Imprimerie Nationale, 1959.

INDIA

Books and Articles

Agrawal, A. N., *Industrial Problems in India,* 3d ed. rev. Delhi, Ranjit, 1956.

Bibliography

Agrawal, Ram Gopal, *Price Controls in India since 1947,* New Delhi, 1956.

Anstey, Vera Powell, *The Economic Development of India,* 4th ed. London and New York, Longmans, Green, 1952.

———, and Taraporevalla, R. J., "Some Aspects of Structure of Indian Industry," *Journal of Royal Statistical Society,* ser. A, *119,* Part I (1956), 62–82.

Balakrishna, Ramachandra, *Measurement of Productivity in Indian Industry,* Economic Series, no. 8, Madras, University of Madras, 1953.

———, *Review of Economic Growth in India,* Bangalore, Bangalore Press, 1961.

Banerji, Sabita (Miss), "The Financial Structure of Small-Scale and Medium-Sized Industries," *Indian Journal of Economics, 38* (1956), 187–95.

Basu, Saroj Kumar, *Industrial Finance in India, A Study in Investment Banking and State-Aid to Industry with Special Reference to India,* 3d ed. Calcutta, University of Calcutta, 1953.

———, *The Managing Agency System in Prospect and Retrospect,* Calcutta, World Press, 1958.

Brimmer, Andrew F., *The Setting of Entrepreneurship in India,* Cambridge, Mass., Center for International Studies, Massachusetts Institute of Technology, 1955.

Calcutta Stock Exchange, *The Stock Exchange, A Symposium,* ed. A. K. Sur, Calcutta, Calcutta Stock Exchange Association, 1958.

Cirvante, V. R., *The Indian Capital Market,* Bombay, Oxford University Press, 1956.

Das, Nabagopal, *Industrial Enterprise in India,* 3d ed. rev. Bombay, Orient Longmans, 1961.

———, *The Public Sector in India,* 2d ed. New York, Asia Publishing House, 1961.

Datta, Bhabadosh, *The Economics of Industrialization,* 2d ed. Calcutta, World Press, 1960.

Davis, Kingsley, *The Population of India and Pakistan,* Princeton, Princeton University Press, 1951.

Dhar, P. N. and Lydal, H. F., *The Role of Small Enterprise in Indian Manufacturing,* Bombay, Asia Publishing House, 1961.

Eddison, John C., *A Case Study in Industrial Development—The Growth of the Pulp and Paper Industry in India,* Cambridge,

Mass., Center for International Studies, Massachusetts Institute of Technology, 1955.

Gadgil, D. R., *Origins of the Modern Indian Business Class, An Interim Report,* New York, Institute of Pacific Relations, 1959.

———, *Planning and Economic Policy in India, 1962,* Gokhale Institute of Politics and Economics, Bombay, Asia Publishing House, 1962.

Great Britain, Board of Trade, Overseas Economic Surveys, *India, Economic and Commercial Conditions in India, 1952,* London, H.M.S.O., 1953.

Gupta, Motilal, *Problems of Unemployment in India,* Rotterdam, 1955.

Hazari, R. K., "Ownership and Control," *Economic Weekly, 12,* Part I (Nov. 26, 1960), 1713–18; Part II (Dec. 3, 1960), 1755–63; Part III (Dec. 10, 1960), 1801–04.

Jain, Prakash Chandra, *Industrial Finance in India,* New Delhi, Suneja Book Center, 1962.

———, *Problems in Indian Economics,* 6th ed. Allahabad, Chaitanya Publishing House, 1960.

Jathar, G. B., and Jathar, K. G., *Indian Economics,* Bombay, Oxford University Press, 1957.

Lamb, Helen B., "The Indian Business Communities and the Evolution of an Industrial Class," *Pacific Affairs, 28* (June, 1955), 101–16.

Lokanathan, Palamadai Samu, "The Indian Economic System" in *Economic Systems of the Commonwealth,* ed. Calvin B. Hoover, Durham, N.C., Duke University Press, 1962.

———, *Industrial Organization in India,* London, Allen and Unwin, 1935.

Mamoria, C. B., *Organization and Financing of Industries in India,* Allahabad, Kitab Mahal, 1960.

Mehta, M. M., *Structure of the Cotton Mill Industry of India,* Allahabad, Friends Book Depot, 1949.

———, *Structure of Indian Industries,* Bombay, Popular Book Depot, 1955.

Munshi, Mantubhai, C., *Industrial Profits in India, 1936–1944; An Inductive Study,* New Delhi, Federation of Indian Chambers of Commerce and Industry, 1948.

187

National Council of Applied Economic Research, *The Managing Agency System,* New Delhi, Asia Publishing House, 1959.

Nigam, Raj K., *Managing Agencies in India (First Round: Basic Facts),* New Delhi, Research and Statistics Division, Department of Company Law, Ministry of Commerce and Industry, 1957.

———, and Chaudhuri, N. C., *The Corporate Sector in India,* New Delhi, Research and Statistics Division, Department of Company Law Administration, Ministry of Commerce and Industry, 1957.

Parekh, H. T., *The Future of Joint-Stock Enterprise in India,* Bombay, Jaico Publishing House, 1958.

Prasad, Kendarnath, *Technological Choice under Development Planning,* Calcutta, Asia Publishing House, 1963.

Rao, Baditha Srinivasa, *Surveys of Indian Industries,* 2 vols. London, Oxford University Press, 1958.

Rosen, George, *Industrial Change in India—Industrial Growth, Capital Requirements and Technological Change, 1937–1955,* Glencoe, Ill., Free Press, 1958.

———, *Some Aspects of Industrial Finance in India,* London, Asia Publishing House, 1962.

Sharma, Tirth Raj, *The Working of State Enterprise in India,* Bombay, Vora, 1961.

Sharma, Tulsi Ram, *Location of Industries in India,* 3d ed. Bombay, Hind Kitabs, 1954.

———, and Chauhan, S. P. Singh, *Indian Industries, Development, Management, Finance and Organization,* Agra, Shiva Lal Agarwala, 1962.

Singh, Pritam, "The Monopoly Problem: Its Implications in India," *Indian Journal of Economics, 39* (1958), 183–90.

Spencer, Daniel L., *India, Mixed Enterprise and Western Business,* The Hague, Martinus Nijhoff, 1959.

U.S. Department of Commerce, Bureau of Foreign Commerce, *Investment in India,* by Celia I. Herman, Washington, D.C., G.P.O., 1961.

U.S. Department of State, Foreign Service despatches for a number of industries from 1961–63.

Vakil, Chandulal Nagindas, *Economic Consequences of Divided India, A Study of the Economy of India and Pakistan,* Bombay, Vora, 1950.

————, and Brahmanand, P. R., *Planning for an Expanding Economy, Accumulation, Employment, and Technical Progress in Underdeveloped Countries,* 1st ed. Bombay, Vora, 1956.

Government Publications

Census Commissioner, *Census of India, 1951,* vol. 1, New Delhi, Government of India Press, 1952.

Central Statistical Organization, *Eleventh Census of Manufactures, India, 1956,* New Delhi, Manager of Publications, 1959.

————, *Monthly Abstract of Statistics,* vol. 16, New Delhi, Manager of Publications, 1963.

————, *Monthly Statistics of the Production of Selected Industries of India,* vols. 12–14, Calcutta, Government of India Press, 1960–63.

Department of Commercial Intelligence and Statistics, *Monthly Statistics of the Foreign Trade of India,* Delhi, Government of India Press, Dec. 1963.

Labour Bureau, *Indian Labour Journal,* vols. 1–4, Delhi, Government of India Press, 1960–63.

————, *Indian Labour Yearbook, 1962,* Delhi, Government of India Press, 1962.

Ministry of Commerce and Industry, *The Journal of Industry and Trade,* vols. 10–12, New Delhi, Directorate of Commercial Publicity, Ministry of Commerce and Industry, 1960–62.

————, *India, Industry and Trade, 1961,* New Delhi, Directorate of Commercial Publicity, Ministry of Commerce and Industry, 1962.

————, *Report of the Ad Hoc Committee on the Automobile Industry,* New Delhi, Manager of Publications, 1960.

Ministry of Information and Broadcasting, *India—A Reference Annual, 1961,* New Delhi, Publications Division, Ministry of Information and Broadcasting, 1961.

————, *Major Industries of India,* New Delhi, 1961.

Planning Commission, *The First Five Year Plan,* New Delhi, Government of India Press, 1953.

————, *Programmes of Industrial Development 1956–1961,* New Delhi, Manager of Publications, 1956.

————, *Second Five Year Plan,* New Delhi, Government of India Press, 1956.

————, *Third Five Year Plan,* New Delhi, Government of India Press, 1961.

————, Scientific and Technical Manpower and Perspective Planning Division, *Occupational Pattern in Manufacturing Industry, 1956,* by Pitamber Pant and M. Basuden, New Delhi, Planning Commission, 1959.

Reserve Bank of India, "Finances of Indian Joint Stock Companies, 1961," *Bulletin,* June 1963, pp. 752–89.

Tariff Commission, *Report on the Continuance of Protection to the Aluminum Industry,* Delhi, Manager of Publications, 1961.

————, *Report on Continuance of Protection to the Sheet Glass Industry,* New Delhi, Manager of Publications, 1960.

————, *Report on the Cost Structure of Sugar, Fair Price Payable to the Sugar Industry,* Delhi, Manager of Publications, 1960.

ITALY

Books and Articles

Associazione Industrie Siderurgiche Italiane, "Assider," *Reportorio delle industrie siderurgiche italiane,* Milan, Industrie Grafiche Italiane Stucchi, 1959.

Banco Commerciale Italiana, Milan, 1961 and 1962. Summary reports for the following companies listed on the Milan Stock Exchange: *Finsider, Dalmine, Terni, Ilva, Italcementi, Montecatini, Società Edison, Cartiere Burgo, Eridania, Snia Viscosa, Saffa, Pirelli.*

Calcatierra, E., Mazzocchi, G., Lombardini, S., and Vito, F., "The Main Outlines of the Structure of the Italian Economy," in *Economic Systems of the West,* ed. R. Frei, Tübingen, J. C. B. Mohr (Paul Siebeck), 2 (1957), 81–119.

Citterio, Carol, Fumagalli, Mario, Turolla, Onelio, (Ufficio Studi delle Acciaierie e Ferriere Lombarde Falck), *Sintesi dell'industria siderurgica italiana nel 1958,* Milan, 1959.

Confederazione Generale dell'Industria Italiana, *Annuario, 1961,* Rome, 1961.

Economic News From Italy, "Italy's 200 Largest Companies," New York, Elite Publishing Company, March, 1962. Other issues were used for 1961 and 1962.

Italy

Fiat, *Report of the Board of Directors and of the Auditors*, balance sheet and operating statements for years ending December 1962 and 1963.

Frumento, Armando, *Nuova Stima del progresso della siderurgia italiana*, Arti-Grafiche Longe e Zoppelli, Padua, 1959.

Italian Institute for Foreign Trade, *Italy Presents*, Rome, 1961 and 1962.

Lucas, Walter, "Finmeccanica" and "Statism in Italy," *Christian Science Monitor*, May 11–14, 1960 and November 9, 1961.

Lutz, Vera, *Italy, A Study in Economic Development*, Royal Institute of International Affairs, London, Oxford University Press, 1962.

Marzan, V. A. "The Experience of Italy," *Economic Consequences of the Size of Nations*, ed. E. A. G. Robinson (New York, St. Martin's Press, 1960), pp. 151–67.

Montecatini, *Report and Balance Sheet, 1960*.

———, *This is Montecatini*, 1960.

Olivetti, *Annual Report, 1960*.

Organizaione Apis, Guida indiriz dell'agricultura italiano, 3d ed. Milan, 1960.

Pirelli, *Gli Stabilimenti Pirelli in Italia*, 1960.

Saraceno, Pasquale, *Rapport sur la situation économique de l'Italie*, Rome, Instituto Poligrafico dello Stato, 1958.

———, *La Situazione economica italiana all'atto dell'entrata in vigore del trattato di Roma*, Rome, Instituto Poligrafico dello Stato, 1958.

———, "Twenty-five Years of Activity of the Instituto per la Ricostruzione Industriale," reprint from Banco di Roma, *Review of Economic Conditions in Italy, 13*, no. 1 (Jan. 1958), Rome.

Società Nazionale Industria Applicazioni Viscosa (Snia Viscosa), *41st Financial Year*, 1958.

———, *Snia Viscoa's 40 Years, 1917–1957*.

Stanford Research Institute, *Economic and Industrial Problems of the Italian Mechanical Industries*, 1951.

Sterling, Claire, "Mattei the Condottiere," *The Reporter*, March 20, 1958.

———, "Professor Valletta and the Fiat Empire," *The Reporter*, April 28, 1960.

Tremelloni, Roberto, *Guida breva delle fonti energetiche in Italia,* Fiera Internazionale di Milano, Milan, 1961.

U.S. Department of State, Foreign Service despatches from 1960–64 pertaining to the following industries: iron and steel, nonferrous metals, motor vehicles, industrial machinery, equipment, chemicals, paper, textiles, and the public sector.

U.S. Mutual Security Agency, Special Mission to Italy for Economic Cooperation, *The Structure and Growth of the Italian Economy,* Rome, 1953.

24 Ore, *Panorama Economico, 1962,* Milan, 1963.

Vito, F., "Monopoly and Competition in Italy," in *Monopoly and Competition and Their Regulation,* ed. Edward H. Chamberlin (London, Macmillan, 1954), pp. 43–60.

Government Publications

Banco di Roma, *Review of Economic Conditions in Italy,* issues of 1960–63.

———, *Ten Years of Italian Economy, 1947–1956,* special issue of the *Review,* 1957.

Ente Nazionale Idrocarburi (E.N.I.), *Annual Report and Statement of Accounts, April 30, 1961,* Rome, 1962.

———, *Energy and Hydrocarbons in 1960,* Rome, 1961.

Instituto Centrali di Statistica, *Annuario statistico italiano, 1962,* Rome, 1963.

———, *Censimento generale dell'industria e del commercio, 1951,* vols. 4–10, Rome, Tip. Failli, 1954.

———, *Statistica Annuale del Commercio con l'Estero, 1956,* Rome, 1958.

Instituto per la Riconstruzione Industriale (I.R.I.), *Annual Report, 1960,* Rome, 1961.

Società Finanziaria Meccanica, *Finmeccanica—Member Companies and Their Products,* Rome, 1961.

———, *Finmeccanica,* Rome, 1958.

Società Finanziaria Siderurgica, *Finsider,* 2d ed. Rome, 1960.

JAPAN

Books and Articles

Abegglen, James C., *The Japanese Factory: Aspects of Its Social Organization,* Glencoe, Ill., Free Press, 1958.

192

Ackerman, Edward A., *Japan's Natural Resources and Their Rela-tion to Japan's Economic Future,* Chicago, University of Chicago Press, 1953.

Ajia Kyokai, *An Outline of Japanese Industry,* Tokyo, Asia Kyokai, 1955.

Allen, George Cyril, *Japan's Economic Recovery,* London and New York, Oxford University Press, 1960.

——, *A Short Economic History of Modern Japan, 1867–1937* (with a supplementary chapter on economic recovery and expansion 1945–60), rev. ed. New York, Praeger, 1963.

——, and Donnithorne, Audrey G., *Western Enterprise in Far Eastern Economic Development, China and Japan,* New York, Macmillan, 1954.

Asian Affairs, 2 (June 1957) (issue on Japanese small business), Tokyo, Asia Kyokai.

Bisson, Thomas Arthur, *Zaibatsu Dissolution in Japan,* Berkeley, University of California Press, 1954.

Cohen, Jerome B., *Japan's Postwar Economy,* Bloomington, Indiana University Press, 1958.

Fairbank, John K., and others, "The Influence of Modern Western Science and Technology on Japan and China," *Explorations in Entrepreneurial History, 7* (1955), 189–204.

Great Britain, Board of Trade, Commercial Relations and Exports Department, *Japan: Economic and Commercial Conditions in Japan,* Overseas Economic Surveys, August 1952, London, H.M.S.O., 1953.

Hadley, Eleanor, "Trust Busting in Japan," *Harvard Business Review,* July 1948, pp. 425–40.

Kazunori, Echigo, "Development of Postwar Japanese Shipbuilding Industry and Revival of Monopoly," *Kyoto University Economic Review, 28* (1958), 35–58.

Levine, Solomon Bernard, *Industrial Relations in Postwar Japan,* Urbana, University of Illinois Press, 1958.

Lockwood, William, *The Economic Development of Japan: Growth and Structural Change 1868–1938,* Princeton, Princeton University Press, 1954.

Okawa, Kazushi, *The Growth Rate of the Japanese Economy since 1878,* Tokyo, Kinokuniya Bookstore, 1957.

Olson, Laurence Alexander, *Dimensions of Japan,* New York, American University Field Staff, 1954.

Oriental Economist, "Cartels in Japan," by Hiroshi Iyori, Jan., 1964.

Oriental Economist, "Zaibatsu Leadership Race," *29,* Part I (February 1961), 73–77; Part II (March 1961), 141–49; Part III (April 1961), 199–202; Part IV (May 1961), 259–63; Part V (June 1961), 350–60.

Rosen, George, "Japanese Industry since the War," *Quarterly Journal of Economics, 67* (1953), 445–63.

Rosovosky, Henry, *Capital Formation in Japan 1868–1940,* Glencoe, Ill., Free Press, 1961.

———, "Japanese Capital Formation: The Role of the Public Sector," *Journal of Economic History, 19* (1959), 350–75.

Rotwein, Eugene, "Economic Concentration and Monopoly in Japan," *Journal of Political Economy, 122* (1964), 262–77.

Schumpeter, Elizabeth Boody, ed., *The Industrialization of Japan and Manchuko 1930–1940: Population, Raw Materials, and Industry,* New York, Macmillan, 1940.

Seki, Kezio, *The Cotton Industry of Japan,* Tokyo, Japan Society for the Promotion of Science, 1956.

Tsuru, Shigetsu, *Essays on Japanese Economy,* Tokyo, Kinokuniya Bookstore, 1958.

U.S. Department of Commerce, Bureau of Foreign Commerce, World Trade Information Service, Part I, Economic Reports, *Basic Data on the Economy of Japan,* September 1958.

———, *Investment in Japan, Basic Information for U.S. Businessmen,* by Saul Baran, Washington, D.C., G.P.O., 1956.

U.S. Department of Commerce, Bureau of International Commerce, Overseas Business Reports, nos. 63–69 (March 1963).

Yamamura, Kozo, "Zaibatsu, Pre-War and Zaibatsu, Postwar," *Journal of Asian Studies, 23* (1964), 539–54.

Government Publications

Economic Planning Agency, *Japanese Economic Statistics,* Tokyo, March 1964.

———, *New Long-Range Economic Plan of Japan 1961–1970, Doubling National Income Plan,* Tokyo, The Japan Times, 1961.

———, Economic Research Institute, *Consumption and Its Degree of Dependence on Imports in Postwar Japan,* Economic Bulletin No. 3, October 1959.

————, *Employment Structure and Business Fluctuations,* Economic Bulletin No. 2, July 1959.

————, *National Income Accounts, 1957, and National Wealth Survey, 1955,* Economic Bulletin No. 1, February 1959.

Fair Trade Commission, unpublished tables on concentration of control by firms in 1958.

Ministry of Finance, *The Annual Returns of the Foreign Trade of Japan, 1956,* Tokyo, 1957.

Ministry of International Trade and Industry, Minister's Secretariat, Research and Statistics Division, *Census of Manufactures, 1956, Report by Industries and Report by Commodities,* vols. 1 and 2, Tokyo, Dec. 1958.

Office of the Prime Minister, Bureau of Statistics, *Monthly Statistics of Japan,* Tokyo, Dec. 1963.

————, *Statistical Yearbook, 1962,* Tokyo, Japan Statistical Association, 1963.

SWEDEN

Books and Articles

Ahrsjö, G. Och and Lagerkvist, C., *Industriproblem 1960,* Stockholm, 1960.

Anstrin, Hans, *Sveriges Pappersindustri,* Stockholm, Engwall and Stråhle, 1951.

Arpi, Gunnar, *Den Svenska Järnhanteringens Träkolsförsörjning,* foreign dissertation, University of Uppsala, 1951.

————, *Sveriges Nutida Näringsliv,* Stockholm, Norstedt, 1958.

Bohman, Clas, *Sveriges Skoindustri,* Stockholm, Industriens Upplysningstjänst, 1949.

Dahmén, Erik, *Svensk Industriell Företagarverksamhet, Kausalanalys auden industriella utveckingen, 1919–1939,* Stockholm, Industriens Utredningsinstitut, 1950.

1947 Års Elbranschkommitté, *Den Svenska Elbranschens Kapacitet Och Konkurrensforhallanden,* vol. 10, Stockholm, Statens Offentliga Utredningar, 1950.

Elinder, Richard Johannes, *Studier I Den Svenska Skoindustrins Struktur,* Stockholm, Almquist and Wiksells, 1948.

Bibliography

Elshult, Alv, and Svennilson, Ingvar, *Kemisk Industri, Karakteristiska Drag, Struktur Och Utvecklingstendenser,* Stockholm, Industriens Utredningsinstitut, 1955.

Hedbom, Olog, *Sveriges Grafiska Industri,* Stockholm, Industriens Upplysningstjänst, 1949.

Hegeland, Hugo, "The Structure and Functioning of Sweden's Political Economy," in *Economic Systems of the West,* ed. R. Frei, Tübingen, J. C. B. Mohr (Paul Siebeck), *1* (1957), 213–42.

Industriens Utredningsinstitut, *Den Svenska Bryggeriindustrin,* Stockholm, 1953.

Lahnhagen, Rolf, *Sveriges Cementindustri,* Stockholm, Engwall and Stråhle, 1950.

Larsson, Bengt, *Den Svenska Porslins-Och Keramikindustrien,* Stockholm, Industriens Upplysningstjänst, 1949.

Nabseth, Lars, *Löneökningars Verkningar Inom Industrin, En Studie av Anpassningsprocessen inom Foretaget,* Stockholm, Almquist and Wicksell, 1961.

Olsson, Ingrid, *Sveriges Slakteriindustri,* Stockholm, Industriens Upplysningstjänst, 1949.

Partsutredningen För Textilindustrien, *Textil-En Industri I Omvandling,* Stockholm, Arbetsmarknad och loner, 1958.

Södra Sveriges Skogsindustriutredning, *Sågverksindustrin I Södra Sverige,* vol. 19, Stockholm, Statens Offentiliga Utredningar, 1953.

Thunaeus, Harold, *Sveriges Bryggeri-Och Läskedrycksindustri,* Stockholm, Industriens Upplysningstjänst, 1953.

Thunell, Bertil, *Sveriges Sågverksindustri,* Stockholm, Industriens Upplysningstjänst, 1959.

Varukistributionsutredningen, *Pris Och Prestation I Handeln,* vol. 16, Stockholm, Status Offentliger Utredningar, 1955.

Government Publications

Kommerskollegium, *1951 Års Företagsrakning, Sveriges Officiella Statistik, Allmanna Ekonomiska Forhallander,* Stockholm, Victor Pettersons Bokindustri Aktiebolog, 1955.
———, *Industri Berättelse För År 1957, Sveriges Officiella Statistik, Industri Och Bergshantering,* Stockholm, Isaac Marcus Boktryckeri Aktiebolag, 1959.

United Kingdom

Statistiska Centralbyran, *Företagens Intäkter, Kostnader Och Vinster År 1957,* Stockholm, K. L. Beckmans Boktruyckeri, 1959.
———, *Statistisk Årsbok För Sverige, 1959,* Stockholm, Kungl. Boktruyckeriet P. A. Norstedt and Soner, 1959.
Sveriges Industriforbund, *Sveriges Industri, 1957,* Stockholm, 1959.

UNITED KINGDOM

Books and Articles

Allen, G. C., "The British Economy," *Economic Systems of the West,* ed. Rudolf Frei, Tübingen, J. C. B. Mohr (Paul Siebeck), *1* (1957), 65–99.
British Iron and Steel Federation, *An Account of the Central Organization in the Steel Industry,* London, B.I.S.F., 1958.
———, *Annual Report, 1958,* London, B.I.S.F., 1959.
British Iron and Steel Quarterly, *Steel, Government and Industry* (reprint from *Steel Review*), London, B.I.S.F., 1958.
———, *Steel Review* (London, B.I.S.F.), nos. 15–17, 1958–60.
British Iron and Steel Research Association, *Annual Report, 1958.*
Burn, Duncan, ed., *The Structure of British Industry,* National Institute of Economic and Social Research, vols. 1 and 2, London, 1959.
Donnithorne, Audrey G., *British Rubber Manufacturing, An Economic Study of Innovations,* London, Duckworth, 1958.
Evely, Richard, and Little, I. M. D., *Concentration in British Industry, An Empirical Study of the Structure of Industrial Production 1935–1951,* Cambridge, Cambridge University Press, 1960.
Florence, P. Sargent, *Post-war Investment, Location and Size of Plant,* National Institute of Economic and Social Research, Occasional Papers 29, Cambridge, Cambridge University Press, 1962.
Hart, P. E., "Business Concentration in the United Kingdom," *Journal of the Royal Statistical Society, 123,* Part 2 (1960), 50–58.
———, and Prais, S. J., "The Analysis of Business Concentration: A Statistical Approach," *Journal of the Royal Statistical Society, 119,* Part 2 (1956), 150–81.

Government Publications

Board of Trade, *Report of the Census of Production, 1954*, vols. 1–12, London, H.M.S.O., 1958.

Central Statistical Office, *Annual Abstract of Statistics, 1962*, London, H.M.S.O., 1963.

Customs and Excise Department, *Annual Statement of the Trade of the United Kingdom, 1954*, vol. 2, London, H.M.S.O., 1955.

Iron and Steel Board, *Annual Report of the Iron and Steel Board for the Year 1958*, London, H.M.S.O., 1959.

———, *Development in the Iron and Steel Industry, Special Report, 1957*, London, H.M.S.O., 1958.

———, *Price Determination, 1960*, no. 1, London, Iron and Steel Board, 1960.

———, and British Iron and Steel Federation, *Annual Statistics, 1958*, London, B.I.S.F., 1959.

UNITED STATES

Books and Articles

Bain, Joe S., *Barriers to New Competition*, Cambridge, Mass., Harvard University Press, 1956.

———, "Relation of Profit Rate to Industry Concentration: American Manufacturing, 1936–1940," *Quarterly Journal of Economics, 65* (1951), 293–324.

Nelson, Ralph L., *Concentration in the Manufacturing Industries of the United States*, New Haven, Yale University Press, 1963.

Shepherd, William G., "Trends of Concentration in American Manufacturing Industries, 1947–1958," *The Review of Economics and Statistics, 66* (1964), 200–12.

Government Publications

U.S. Department of Commerce, Bureau of the Census, *Census of Manufactures, 1954*, vol. 1, *Summary Statistics*, Washington, D.C., G.P.O., 1955.

———, *Census of Population, 1960, Summary Statistics*, Washington, D.C., G.P.O., 1961.

U.S. Department of the Interior, Bureau of Mines, *Petroleum Refineries, Including Cracking Plants, in the United States, Jan. 1,*

1959, by C. E. Hennig, Information Circular 7937, Washington, D.C., G.P.O., 1959.

U.S. Senate, Committee on the Judiciary, Subcommittee on Antitrust and Monopoly, *Concentration in American Industry,* Washington, D.C., G.P.O., 1957.

GENERAL REFERENCES

Buxbaum, Richard, "Anti-Trust Regulation within the European Economic Community," *Columbia Law Review, 61* (1961), 402–09.

Food and Agricultural Organization, Statistics Division, *Fertilizers: A World Report on Production and Consumption,* Rome, F.A.O., 1960.

———, *Production Yearbook, 1962,* Rome, F.A.O., 1963.

———, *Trade Yearbook, 1962,* Rome, F.A.O., 1963.

International Labor Office, *Yearbook of Labor Statistics, 1962,* Geneva, I.L.O., 1962.

Kuznets, Simon; Moore, Wilbert E; Spengler, Joseph J., eds., *Economic Growth, Brazil, India and Japan,* Durham, N.C., Duke University Press, 1955.

Lister, Louis, *Europe's Coal and Steel Community,* New York, Twentieth Century Fund, 1960.

Oil and Gas Journal, March 31 and Dec. 28, 1959. (Data on petroleum refinery capacity.)

Organization for European Economic Cooperation, *The Pulp and Paper Industry in Europe, Developments between 1950 and 1957, The Situation in 1958, Prospects for 1963–1965,* Paris, O.E.E.C., 1959.

———, Chemical Committee, *Trends in Economic Sectors: The Chemical Industry in Europe, 1954,* and *1959/60,* Paris, O.E.E.C., 1961.

———, Iron and Steel Committee, *Trends in Economic Sectors: The Iron and Steel Industry in Europe, 1955, 1956/57,* and *1958/59,* Paris, O.E.E.C., 1958, 1960.

———, Non-Ferrous Metals Committee, *Trends in Economic Sectors: The Non-Ferrous Metal Industry in Europe, 1957,* Paris, O.E.E.C., 1958.

———, Oil Committee, *Trends in Economic Sectors: Oil, Recent Development in O.E.E.C. Area, 1957,* Paris, O.E.E.C., 1958.

———, Textile Committee, *Trends in Economic Sectors, The Textile Industry in Europe, 1953, 1955/56,* and *1958/59,* Paris, O.E.E.C., 1958, 1960.

Robinson, E. A. G., ed., *Economic Consequences of the Size of Nations* (proceedings at conference held by International Economic Association), New York, St. Martin's Press, 1960.

Scitovsky, Tibor, *Economic Theory and Western European Integration,* London, Allen and Unwin, 1958.

Stocking, George W., and Watkins, Myron W., *Cartels and Competition,* New York, Twentieth Century Fund, 1948.

United Nations, Statistical Office, *Statistical Papers, Series D,* New York, Jan.–Dec. 1954.

———, Department of Economic and Social Affairs, *Statistical Yearbook, 1957,* and *1962,* New York, 1957 and 1962.

INDEX

Index

Dual structure, 98. *See also* Dual economies

Dunlop, 79

Economic: development, 85, 134; growth, 106; performance, 4, 6 ff.; planning, 94, 107

Economies of scale, 59, 66, 124, 133, 145, 150. *See also* Optimal scale; Plant: size, efficient

Efficiency: comparative industry, 8, 26, 56, 134; comparative plant, 55–56, 136; plant, 57 ff., 124

Eight countries, 7; company-plant concentration multiples, 132–33; composition of manufacturing activity, 23; industry employment, 31; industrial structure, 8, 11, 134–55; industrialization, 13, 17; national economic structure, 13; plant concentration, 34, 42–55, 127–28; plant efficiency, 58–66; plant size, 34, 38–42; population, 12; seller concentration, 71–75, 119–22, 127–28

Electric: cables and conduits industry, 101; wire and cable industry, 88

Electrical: equipment industry, 88, 101; household appliances industry, 88; machinery industry, 100, 102

Electricity industry, 99

Electronic equipment industry, 100 ff.

Employment, 9, 11–13, 27; agriculture, 17; as seller concentration measure, 74, 103; Canada, 31; commerce, 17; construction, 17, 118; disguised, 42; explosives industry, 31; firm size measure, 67–68; hardware industry, 31; India, 23, 31; industry, 22, 29, 34, comparative, 18, 31, 42, 46, U.S., 57; Italy, 60–61; manufacturing, 17, 23, 118, comparative, 141; mining, 118; plant, as concentration measure, 10, 24, 57, 126, 129, as size measure, 25, 41, 60, comparative, 42, efficient, 61, inefficient, 66, 141; pulp industry, 31; seafood industry, 31; services, 17; shipbuilding, 31; sugar refining, 31; tobacco products industry, 31; U.K., 31; U.S., 31, 57, 61; wool textiles industry, 31; wood pulp industry, 31

Engine industry, 101

Engineering industry, 98–100 passim

Ente Nazionale Idrocarburi (E.N.I.), 99

Entry, conditions, 10. *See also* Barriers

Environment, business, 134

Estimation procedure, 27–30, 35

Evely, Richard, 76

Excess of company over plant concentration, 123, 126

Explosives industry, 31

Export promotion, 85

Export-Import Trading Law (Japanese, *1952*), 86 n.

Extractive industry, 106. *See also* Mining

Fabricated metal products industry, 19, 23

Far East, 42

Farm machinery industry, 100, 102

Fertilizer industry, 85, 99

Fiat, 101

Financing system, 87

Fincantieri, 99

Finelettrica, 99

Finished products, 88

Finmare, 99
Finmeccanica, 99
Finsider, 99
Firm: definition, 73; number, 67, 69, 124; size, 74, comparative, 141, distribution of, 67, 69, 77 n., 124 *(see also* Concentration: seller); largest, 68 ff.
Flour industry, 96, 107
Food industry, 19, 23, 84, 88, 98
Fossil fuel industry, 19
Foreign ownership, 105. *See also* Concentration: increasing forces
France, 90–96; cartels, 94–95; general planning commission, 94; government enterprise, 95; government policy, 95; government regulation, 94; import competition, 96; manufacturing sector, 95; mergers, 94–95; seller concentration, 90–96; super-control groups, 95
Free-enterprise economies, 6, 80, 112

General Planning Commission, French, 94
Geographical area, 3, 105
Geography, 40, 102. *See also* Concentration: increasing forces
Glass industry, 88, 98, 106
Government: antitrust policy, 74, 102, 120 ff., 135, 151 ff., 154, Canada, 154, France, 95, India, 115, 121, Italy, 99, Japan, 85, 90, Sweden, 118–19 *(see also* Antitrust policy); licensing, 147; monopolies, 84, 86, 91, 94 ff., 111; participation in enterprise, 9, 74, 102, 121, 135, 147–48, Canada, 105–06, France, 95, India, 110, Italy, 99–100, Sweden, 118, U.K., 80, U.S., 80; regulation of indus-

try, 7, 73, 121 ff., 135, Canada, 105, France, 94, India, 111–12, Italy, 98, Japan, 84–85, Sweden, 118, U.K., 80
Grain products industry, 31

Hardware industry, 31
Heavy industry. *See* Industry: heavy
Holding company, 81, 86 ff., 115, 135 *(see also* Influence groups; Managing agencies; Super-control groups); government, 99, 121
Horizontal integration, 90, 102, 113 ff., 120–21, 147, 152–53. *See also* Monopoly; Oligopoly
Household industry, 22 ff. *See also* Cottage industry; Traditional industry

Import competition, 9, 74, 122, 135; Canada, 105–06; France, 96; India, 115–16; Italy, 102; Japan, 90; Sweden, 119; U.K., 80–81
Income distribution effects, 115
Income, per capita, 17
Incorporation, 112
India, 106–16; census of manufactures, 23; commerce and service sectors, 18 n.; cottage industry, 22; employment, 18, 22 ff., 31–32; food industry, 23; government enterprise, 110; government policy, 115, 121; government regulation, 111–12; import competition, 115–16; industry diversification, 23; labor surplus, 18; leather industry, 23; licensing committee, 111; lumber industry, 23; manufacturing, 22 ff.; monopoly, 115; nonmetallic industry (mineral products), 23; saw and planing mills industry,

Index

31; seller concentration, 106–16; sugar refining industry, 31; super-control groups, 112; tobacco products industry, 31

Indian Companies Act, 114

Industrial: chemicals industry, 99; development, 3, 6, 18; diversification, 22 ff., 34; machinery industry, 100; performance, 5; production, 7, 61; sectors, 3; structure, 3–6 passim, comparative, 7 ff., 134–55 (*see also* Structure)

Industrialization, 3, 6, 13, 40, 134

Industry: capacity, 111 (*see also* Capacity; Output); classification, 30 ff., 69, 71; comparative size, 148 (*see also* Size); composition, 38; heavy, 84, 90, 102, 107, 120, 139

Inflation, 94

Influence groups, 95–96. *See also* Managing agencies; Super-control groups; Zaibatsu

Instituto per la Ricostruzione (I.R.I.), 99

Insurance industry, 88

Investment, 6, 94 ff.; government influence on, 101; requirements, 94

Iron and Steel Board, British, 80

Iron and steel industries, 19

Iron curtain countries, 6

Italy, 96–103; cartels, 98–99; Central Price Commission, 98; concentration measures, 50; employment, 60–61; government enterprise, 99–100; government policy, 99; government regulation, 98; import competition, 102; monopoly, 101; oligopoly, 98, 101; plant size, 60–61; seller concentration, 96–102; soap industry, 60–61; super-control groups, 101 ff.

Japan, 4 n., 81–90; Anti-Monopoly Law, 85; cartels, 85–86; commerce and service sectors, 18 n.; employment, 18, 31; Export-Import Trading Law, 86 n.; government policy, 85, 90; government regulation, 84–85; household industry, 22; import competition, 90; labor surplus, 18; manufacturing, 22; mergers, 85–90; Ministry of International Trade and Industry, 86 n.; monopoly, 84, 86, 90; oligopoly, 84, 89; seller concentration, 81–90; Smaller Enterprise Stabilization Act, 86 n.; super-control groups, 87, 113 (*see also* Zaibatsu)

Japanese Fair Trade Commission, 83

Labor: intensity, 42; intensive production, 60; productivity, 6, 17, 41 ff.; surplus, 18 n.

Language barrier, 4 n.

Largest plants. *See* Plant size

Lead industry, 81, 90, 102

Leather industry, 23

Les 500 Premières Sociétés Françaises, 91

Licensing Committee, Indian, 111

Little, I. M. D., 76

Location, 111

Lumber industry, 19, 23

Machine tool industry, 88, 96, 100 ff., 116

Machinery industry, 19, 88

Managerial remuneration, 112

Managing agencies, 9, 112, 114 ff.

Index

Index